ACCOUNTING AND FINANCE PRACTICE SERIES

Merging Your CPA Firm

A Guide to Successful Acquisition or Sale of an Accounting Practice

Robert J. Gallagher, CPA
President, R.J. Gallagher & Associates, Inc.

GOVERNORS STATE UNIVERSITY
UNIVERSITY PARK
IL 60466

SHEPARD'S/McGRAW-HILL, INC.
P.O. Box 1235
Colorado Springs, Colorado 80901

McGRAW-HILL BOOK COMPANY
New York ● St. Louis ● San Francisco ● Auckland ● Bogotá ● Caracas
Colorado Springs ● Hamburg ● Lisbon ● London ● Madrid ● Mexico
Milan ● Montreal ● New Delhi ● Oklahoma City ● Panama ● Paris
San Juan ● São Paulo ● Singapore ● Sydney ● Tokyo ● Toronto

1234567890 SHLB 897654321098

Library of Congress Cataloging-in-Publication Data

Gallagher, Robert J.
  Merging your CPA firm: a guide to successful acquisition
or sale of an accounting practice/
  Robert J. Gallagher.
      p. cm. — (Accounting and finance practice series)
  Includes index.
  ISBN 0-07-172153-3
      1. Accounting firms—Reorganization. 2. Consolidation and
merger of corporations. I. Title. II. Series.
HF5627.G36 1988
657'.068—dc19   88-15652
                                                          CIP

ISBN 0-07-172153-3

Shepard's Accounting and Finance Practice Series

To my family and mentors
for their patience and guidance

Foreword

Merger mania is sweeping the business world today and CPA firms are part of this syndrome. Recent surveys reveal a continuing merging trend within the CPA profession. Along with a higher instance of mergers among CPA firms within the past 10 years, results indicate a continuing desire to merge. The competition created by deregulation is a factor strongly influencing this desire, that is to say, necessity is motivating the mania as much as the traditional concern with growth. The survival of many firms may depend on making a sound merger.

Obviously, the combined strengths of two firms can form a bigger, better, and more profitable unit. Unfortunately, however, merging does not guarantee success. The disaster of a failed merger all too readily attests to the risk involved. It is a difficult and irrevocable process, the success of which requires careful consideration of many factors.

When I went through the merger process, the only sources of information I could refer to were some articles in a professional publication and the material that appeared in the management section of an accounting practice handbook. Seeing the need for solid reference material, we decided to develop a handbook offering guidance to others seeking information on merging. Whether you are considering selling, combining, or acquiring an accounting firm, this handbook is for you.

This handbook contains a comprehensive account of merging. It offers its reader quality counsel based on professional expertise. The handbook is divided into chapters which are arranged systematically, allowing for easy reference to the many stages of the merging process. At the end of each chapter there is a suggested reading list. Examples of actual merger documents are contained in many chapters and answers to frequently asked questions appear at the end of certain chapters. Following are some of the many issues addressed in the handbook:

How "merger mania" has affected the CPA profession.

What are the primary reasons for merging? What are the advantages and disadvantages of a merger or acquisition?

What are the initial meeting considerations? What are the objectives to be determined in engineering a merger?

Learn negotiation strategies. Review an example of a prospective merger questionnaire.

How to value an accounting practice.

Preparation of the "merger report card."

The role of human resources in determining the success or failure of a merger.

How to prepare for a merger by solid business planning.

We sincerely hope that you find this handbook useful in providing the information you need for the merger process.

Robert J. Gallagher, CPA

Contents

Summary

Detailed

Overview of the Merging Syndrome

1

The best introduction to merger can be gained by presenting an overview of the CPA profession during the past 10 years. By looking at recent merging trends among CPA practices it is possible to arrive at the principal reasons for merging and, also, to determine the effects of the merging process. We can, in short, learn by example. Recently, I read an article, which appeared in the June, 1932 issue of *Fortune Magazine*, about certified public accountants. It was interesting to note that, of the 20 largest CPA firms mentioned in that article, only Price Waterhouse, Arthur Andersen, and Arthur Young & Co. have not had a name change during the past 56 years. Mergers have always been a way of life since the profession started, and merger madness will always be part of our profession. A firm with excellent professionals will always be a target of larger firms.

The atmosphere in the CPA profession has been chaotic ever since the American Institute of CPAs lifted its ban on advertising in 1978. In March 1979, because of potential antitrust problems, the council of the AICPA repealed the encroachment and solicitation ban. Normally, deregulation breeds efficiency, but this had *not* been the effect on our profession. Deregulation has created havoc for many CPA firms throughout the country. The number of new firms that have entered the CPA market in the past 10 years has resulted in additional competition. Also, increases in professional liability insurance, staff turnover, and a blizzard of professional pronouncements have all contributed to the difficulty that CPA firms are having managing their practices. These are the issues that lead many firms to ask, "Should we sellout?" Well-managed firms are promptly acquiring those firms that do sellout, and at bargain prices. Generally, firms are seeking to determine the best way to proceed during the next decade. Even the large national firms are considering mergers.

While merger mania has swept through the entire business world, it is now prevalent in the CPA profession. Many of the larger firms grew as a result of acquiring smaller practices throughout the country. Today merging is a topic on the agenda of most CPA firms—large or small. As previously mentioned, many CPA firms are experiencing an erosion in earnings and facing increased competition. These factors hinder the operation of a firm and present significant problems for its management. Partners in medium-sized CPA firms are so frustrated that they think an upstream merger may be the answer. Administrative requirements, fiduciary responsibilities, and performance pressures become so great that many firms seek a solution in merging. Well, it is not the entire answer—the grass is not always greener. While many firms do eliminate some of their problems by merging, they soon see that they are also facing new problems.

When one looks at the list of second-tier firms of 20 years ago, most of the names have now disappeared as the result of either mergers or dissolution. Many partners in those firms agree in retrospect that the merger activity within the firms was not properly planned. From this list, it is quite evident that all firms, except Seidman & Seidman, have experienced a name change or have merged with other firms:

Alexander Grant & Company

Laventhol, Krekstein, Horwath & Horwath

Main Lafrentz Co.

Elmer Fox & Company

Seidman & Seidman

S.D. Leidesdorf & Co.

J.K. Lasser & Co.

Harris, Kerr, Forster

McGladrey, Hansen, Dunn

Hurdman and Cranstown Penny & Co

Wolf & Company

A.M. Pullen & Company[1]

When one compares this list with the top second-tier firms of 1988, it is quite evident that many of the above firms have merged with other firms. Merger activity has been a way of life ever since our great profession started. The following chart appeared in an early 1988 issue of the *Accounting Office Management & Administration Report:* [2]

Table 1. Second-tier firms

Firm

Laventhol & Horwath

Grant Thornton

McGladrey Hendrickson
 & Pullen

Seidman & Seidman

Kenneth Laventhal

Pannell Kerr Forster

Spicer & Oppenheim

The following list of firms represent the third tier

Firm

Baird, Kurtz & Dobson

Plante & Moran

Crowe Chizek & Co

Moss Adams

Cherry, Bekaert & Holland

Clifton Gunderson & Co

Altschuler, Melvoin and Glasser

J.H. Cohn & Company

Richard A. Eisner & Company

Mann Judd Landau

---

[1] McGladrey, Hansen & Dunn merged with Hendrickson Company to form McGladrey, Hendrickson, and then merged with A.M. Pullen to form McGladrey, Hendrickson & Pullen.

[2] Acct Off Mgmt & Admin Rep issue 88-3 (Mar 1988).

The present group of second-tier firms is a group of energetic and dynamic firms. They are also confronting the decision of continued growth through mergers.

In September 1985, several articles appeared, written by Lee Berton, a staff reporter of the *Wall Street Journal*, regarding the potential merger of Peat Marwick and KMG Main Hurdman. On September 25, 1985, Berton wrote an article about the termination of merger discussions between the two firms. "The two companies apparently couldn't resolve a raft of complex issues that included how to structure the new firm, persons familiar with the talks said."[3]

In the August 1986 issue of the *Public Accounting Report*,[4] an article described how Laventhol Horvath replaced KMG Main Hurdman as the ninth largest CPA firm. The article also stated that KMG Main Hurdman was experiencing bottom-line problems. It should be noted that, in 1979, KMG Main Hurdman was formed by a merger of Hurdman & Cranstoun and Main La Frentz. In 1983 they considered merging with Alexander Grant & Company, which at that time was the nation's 10th largest United States accounting firm, but the merger fell through. Apparently KMG Main Hurdman, with its strong international organization, was still looking for a partner, and on January 1, 1987, the firm finally did merge with Peat Marwick Mitchell & Co. The new name is Peat, Marwick, Main & Co.

Deloitte Haskins & Sells and Price Waterhouse almost went to the altar, but then decided to terminated merger negotiations in December 1984, at the last minute, because of the lack of approval of the partners in the British international organization. Both firms realized how difficult it is to combine large operations which require the approval of their international affiliates. At that time I was a partner with Deloitte Haskins & Sells and know the frustration and anguish of many partners when the merger talks were terminated. Everyone thought it was a "done deal." It would have combined two well-managed firms into one excellent organization.

Most of the top twenty-five CPA firms have developed strategic plans regarding their merger activity. In fact, it would not be surprising if two of the Big Eight firms merged before the end of the year.

The merger activity discussed above must be considered along with the entrepreneurial spirit—the spirit that gives every young CPA the opportunity to start his or her own practice and to build a firm, as many

---

[3] Berton, *Peat Marwick and KMG Main Hurdman Terminate Exploratory Merger Talks*, Wall St. J., Sept. 25, 1985, at __, col __. See also **apps 1-1 to 1-4**.

[4] *KMG Main Hurdman Tightens Belt to Improve Profitability*, vol. IX Pub Acct Rep 1 (Arthur W Bowman, ed Aug 1986).

others have during their lifetimes. The significant increase in the number of CPA firms practicing, together with projections that these numbers will be substantially larger in the next decade, make it extremely important for each firm to determine its course of action in the merger arena and to adopt a firm philosophy. A decision whether to merge or enter an acquisition program should be part of any firm's business plan. However, it is extremely important for a firm that decides to proceed on a merger and acquisition route to learn from examples of the past.

Clarence Rainess & Company was a 50-partner, $13 million firm that eventually dissolved in July of 1978. J.K. Lasser merged with Touche Ross and Company in 1977, and today there are very few J.K. Lasser partners in the Touche Ross organization. Lester Witte and Company was a growing company which eventually filed for bankruptcy to protect its shareholders. Wolf & Co. was another company that experienced financial problems. These four are all examples of firms that grew via the merger route and then, except for isolated offices, all but disappeared.

When Lester Witte encountered problems, it decided to reorganize under Chapter 11 of the Bankruptcy Act. This particular bankruptcy was the result of a number of bad decisions in the merger process. Different decisions were made for different acquisitions—all of a sudden everyone attends the same party and finds out that one firm's deal was different from the others. At one time it had been one of the 25 largest firms in the country.

Clarence Rainess is another firm that was among the top 25 CPA firms in the nation; after years of growth, it started to suffer a profit slump and a loss of clientele. Clarence Rainess was an old-line New York City firm specializing in bankruptcy proceedings, and it lost several key partners, including a managing partner. Eventually, the partners executed a dissolution agreement and, again, the dreams of many were destroyed because of poor management and also because they crossed a threshold they were not prepared for. There is no question that a firm that wants to grow can do so in an efficient manner, but it must have strong leadership, especially in today's turbulent times.

While J.K. Lasser Company was growing, it acquired practices and, because of substantial retirement obligations and high professional liability insurance premiums, it decided to merge with Touche Ross & Company. Today, there are very few J.K. Lasser partners left in the Touche Ross organization, because the merger was consummated too quickly without enough consideration of the philosophies of both firms. In retrospect, it was a merger that should not have been consummated.

Seidman & Seidman is another accounting firm whose members sometimes shudder when they remember the early 1970s, because that is when Seidman acquired Wolfson, Weiner and Company, a small Los Angeles-based accounting firm whose principal client was Equity Funding Corporation of America. Approximately one year later, Equity Funding collapsed and fraud was uncovered involving not only the CPA firm (Weiner & Co.), but also the management of the company. It was a very difficult period for all partners in the firm and specifically for the current chairman of the board of Seidman & Seidman, Mr. John D. Abernathy. However, since then Seidman & Seidman has still shown interest in growing via the merger route; since 1985 Seidman has acquired several accounting firms, increasing its revenue and becoming the 11th largest firm in the United States. A great lesson was learned when a merger of a small firm almost destroyed the entire credibility of Seidman & Seidman. It can be compared to the unfortunate situation that occurred with Grant Thornton & Company, when a partner committed a criminal act that almost destroyed the reputation of the entire firm.

These two examples send the message that, in any merger, it is extremely important to perform an audit of the firm to be acquired. The larger firms have task forces that work on mergers. They require an entire review of the CPA firm's files and quality controls before a merger will be approved. The smaller firms do not have such departments. However, I recommend that such firms definitely consult with an outside consultant knowledgeable in the CPA profession and with the merger arena.

Another firm that grew to be a large medium-sized firm was Wolf & Co. This firm made some good business decisions in retiring nonperforming partners, but at an extremely high cost. With increased liability insurance costs, together with retirement commitments and other expenses, the firm dissolved in 1978 into several practices. Obviously, the litigation climate intensified as many retired partners who did not receive their distributions filed suit. After a number of years in court and substantial legal fees, there was a settlement, but many of the retired partners realized very little in comparison to the effort it had taken to build their practice.

In this age of competition, it is not surprising that firms such as Lester Witte, J.K. Lasser, Clarence Rainess, and Wolf & Co. had difficulties. These difficulties, however, have left scars on those individuals who had worked very hard to form their organizations. Some of these firms, for example, acquired many smaller practices with the agreement that the merged partners would be included in the firm's *unfunded* retirement plan. Naturally, there were many frustrated and angry partners when these firms dissolved, particularly those who were admitted via the merger route. It is instructive to consider the number of firms that merge their practices, encounter difficulties, and eventually end up frustrated and with very little to show for their long years of hard work.

In the December 1987 issue of the *Bowman's Accounting Report,* the editor discusses the details of how Fox & Company was saved from bankruptcy when former partners gave up retirement benefits and capital payments to help the firm avoid bankruptcy. The editor relays the following account:

> "The present value of my capital balance wouldn't buy me a glass of iced tea," says former Fox & Company regional partner David Vink, now managing partner of Vink Pier & Teague, Dallas. Fox's liabilities exceed assets by more than $3 million as of March 31, 1987, according to documents *Bowman's* has obtained.
>
> Former Fox partners are giving up retirement benefits and capital payments to help the firm avoid bankruptcy.
> "That was the unknown—What happens in bankruptcy?," asks William Dent, Fox Chairman. "That's what we were trying to avoid. That's what we were working toward. The (restructuring) plan was approved. The deal was closed June 30."
> Fox was purported to have merged into Grant Thornton. "There never was a merger," Dent says. "I don't know what (re-tired partners) understood. They were given information about the combination."
>
> Fox ceased operations May 1, 1985, and 135 of its partners took practice thought to be valued at almost $75 million to Grant. Grant agreed to pay those partners $22 million over 20 years, much of the money going to Fox to pay retirement benefits.
> Retired Fox partners have been getting only 80% of their month-ly benefits. That changes shortly. Of three options offered:
> - 28% took a cash lump sum payment worth 50% of benefits, which were already discounted 10%
> - 17% opted for 65% of benefits over their normal life, without being subject to any offsets by Grant or Fox
> - 55% went for 80% of benefits over their normal life at the

risk of offsets by Grant or Fox for any retired partner litigation expenses.[5]

It should also be noted that, as some of the aforementioned firms grew, they realized that they had to have all the departments of a national firm but did not have adequate financial resources to sustain their growth. In other words, they crossed various thresholds but eventually came to a threshold that could not be crossed.

On a positive note, we should point out that many fine practices existing today came out of the breakup of some of the firms that dissolved; such practices are obviously very careful when it comes to mergers and acquisitions. There have also been some very good mergers from a strategic viewpoint. For example, in considering the unlikely merger in 1978 of Ernst & Ernst with S.D. Leidesdorf, a New York-based second-tier firm, the benefits derived by Ernst & Ernst from the merger included obtaining a representation of clientele in retail, textile, and real estate fields, in addition to its own strength in the banking, insurance, and healthcare industries. Furthermore, the merger provided Ernst & Ernst with a greater ability to penetrate the lucrative New York market, in which their office was the smallest of the Big Eight.

Although we have just reviewed some negative experiences of firms in the merger process, we must not overlook those firms that have executed very successful mergers. Many firms engineer mergers with excellent results, but such firms have done their homework and have established sound merger plans. Today, it is very important for firms to develop a merger report card and seek outside counsel. We shall discuss these factors in more detail in subsequent chapters. Mark Stevens discusses the merger success of the CPA firm of Israeloff, Trattner & Company in his book, *The Accounting Wars*. He attributes their success to sound merger strategy:

> "From my perspective, the really important thing was that Dad and I had stumbled onto a fundamental law of the accounting marketplace: that an established practice could be transferred from one principal to another with no loss of business. I knew there was something to that, some way to profit from that lesson."
>
> That "way" turned out to be a simple but brilliant strategy for building a substantial and highly profitable accounting practice. . . ."

Over the years, Israeloff's deals have followed a fairly standard formula. Typically, he pays the principal or the heirs a multiple

---

[5] *Fox & Company Saved from Bankruptcy as Former Partners Cut Benefits*, Bowman's Acct Rep (July 1987) (reprinted with permission).

of one to two times gross fees, with 10 to 20 percent down and the balance over four to five years. The earliest deals, negotiated when there was less competition for small accounting practices, were especially sweet, with the purchase multiple rarely exceeding 1.5 (closer to 2.0 today) and with no interest due on the payout. In addition, Israeloff allocated only a small part (an average of 10 percent) of the purchase price to goodwill, thus enabling him to deduct virtually the full amount of the investment.

To protect himself against major client defections jeopardizing recently completed acquisitions, Israeloff built a provision into the purchase agreements providing for a debit of one and a half times[6] the client fee for all clients leaving Israeloff Trattner within two years of the acquisition.

Starting off as he does with a propitious purchase price and then covering his risk from all directions. Israeloff is virtually assured of a successful acquisition. His twenty-three-year buying and merging spree has produced a string of thirty-seven deals that have nurtured his firm's bottom line and, even more important, have fulfilled the master plan he concocted as an ambitious young man.

"I always viewed the merger and acquisition strategy as a means to an end," he says. "That being the establishment of a sufficient fee and client base to achieve considerable internal growth, to invest in staff and technology, and to compete with virtually any firm, of any size."[7]

Mr. Stevens also reviews the growth of Laventhol & Horwath, which went through 41 mergers between 1968 to 1971. In 1980 it initiated a second round of 30 mergers. In their initial merger sweep they encountered several problems and spent the next nine years solidifying the organization before undertaking the next series of mergers. Under the leadership of George Bernstein, the firm has now positioned itself as one of the top second-tier firms.

Clifton, Gundersen & Co. is a regional firm with several offices in the Midwest. This firm has been successful in growing via the merger route. Its success can be attributed to a sound merger policy and excellent firm leadership. There are other firms I have not mentioned that also have been successful in the merger process. All such firms have developed a "merger policy" as part of their business plan.

---

[6] The same multiple is used to price the practice.

[7] M. Stevens, The Accounting Wars 181-83 (1985). Reprinted with permission of Macmillan Publishing Company from Accounting Wars by Mark Stevens. Copyright © 1985 by Mark Stevens.

As firms grow, they cross various thresholds and must be able to meet the challenges involved. Anticipating these challenges is the first step in overcoming them. For various reasons some of the aforementioned firms were not successful in doing this. Strategic planning is an important part of the merger process. The purpose of this handbook is to provide information that will assist CPA partners and managers in preparing a merger plan for their firm. It is extremely important, for example, to look at management when considering an upstream merger candidate. As previously mentioned, a strong managing partner is crucial to the future growth and profitability of today's CPA firms. Such considerations will be treated systematically in subsequent chapters of this handbook.

When you are considering being acquired by another firm, you must be very careful to ascertain that the acquiring firm is stable, is in strong financial condition, and has excellent management. If this is the first step in the merger arena[1] for both firms, then you should be very cautious and take the time to execute an effective merger.

In the next chapter, we will discuss why firms merge and the related advantages and disadvantages.

Selected Reading List

Berton, *CPA Firms Diversify, Cut Fees, Steal Clients In Battle for Business,* Wall St J, Sept 20, 1985, at 1, col 4.

Berton, *Though Once Bitten, Abernathy Isn't Shy,* Wall St J, May 15, 1987, at 34, col 1.

Ernst & Ernst/Leidesdorf Merger, 1 Pub Acct Rep 1 (Arthur W Bowman ed, Aug 1978).

Fox & Company Saved from Bankruptcy as Former Partners Cut Benefits, Bowman's Acct Rep (Arthur W. Bowman ed, July 1987).

Istvan, *Merger Mania—Why?,* vol 9, no 5 Practicing CPA 7 (May 1985).

Lester Witte Files for Chapter 11 Bankruptcy, 5 Pub Acct Rep 1 (Arthur W Bowman ed, 1982).

Local Firms Want to Buy Other Local Firms for New Services, 7 Pub Acct Rep 1 (Arthur W Bowman ed, 1984).

Second Tier May Be More of a Threat Than The Big Eight, Acct Off Mgmt Admin Rep issue 88-3 (David Foster ed, Mar 1988).

M. Stevens, The Accounting Wars (1985).

---

[1] McGladrey, Hansen & Dunn merged with Hendrickson Company to form McGladrey, Hendrickson, and then merged with A.M. Pullen to form McGladrey, Hendrickson & Pullen.

What's Left of Clarence Rainess and Company, 1 Pub Acct Rep 11 (Arthur W Bowman ed, 1978).

Total War

CPA Firms Diversify, Cut Fees, Steal Clients In Battle for Business

'The White Gloves Are Off' As Revenue Is Squeezed; Peat Marwick's Bloodbath

Will Audits' Quality Suffer?

By Lee Berton
Staff Reporter of The Wall Street Journal

KMG Main Hurdman, the ninth-biggest U.S. accounting firm, has a service that analyzes commercial ventures in outer space. Laventhol & Horwath, the 11th biggest, recently plugged one of its newsletters by offering potential subscribers cameras, clocks and travel guides. Laventhol also owns an outfit called Index, which designs hotel interiors.

Is this any way to run an accounting firm?

As recently as the 1970s, accounting firms had only a handful of products—auditing, tax work, estate planning and management consulting. And a clublike camaraderie prevailed: Most firms wouldn't be caught dead swiping a competitor's client. Because there was plenty of business to go around, firms sat back and waited for clients to come to them.

But the profession has been thrust into a new competitive world of survival. Corporate merger mania has shrunk the pool of clients. Rates for malpractice insurance have tripled. Firms now are scraping for every piece of business by cutting auditing fees and branching into areas that often have little direct connection with accounting. And stealing clients has become a way of life.

Then and Now

"Five years ago if a client of another firm came to me and complained about the service, I'd immediately warn the other firm's chief executive," says J. Michael Cook, the chairman of Deloitte, Haskins & Sells, the nation's No. 7 accounting firm. "Today I try to take away his client."

Says Arthur Bowman, the editor of the Public Accounting Report,

---

an Atlanta newsletter: "Today almost anything that makes money goes."

But the trend disturbs many in the profession, government and the academic world. They worry that firms may get so cutthroat that they will fall down on what many see as their primary duty: independently auditing the books of publicly held companies. The biggest potential loser is the public, these critics argue.

"The increased aggressiveness of firms in selling their services is bound to lead to erosion in the quality of the audit," says Loyd Heath, a professor of accounting at the University of Washington in Seattle.

House Panel's Inquiry

A House subcommittee headed by Rep. John Dingell, Democrat of Michigan, has been holding hearings on the accounting profession since last February. The hearings were prompted by a belief that accounting firms had been too quick to give clean bills of health to banks, thrifts, securities firms and other companies that subsequently collapsed. "We're very concerned that the more hats an accounting firm wears for its clients, the more the firm is in the client's pocket," says Michael Barrett, the subcommittee's chief counsel.

Clearly there is a revenue squeeze in the profession, and it is taking a human toll. Revenues at the eight largest firms grew a total of only 22% over the past two years, down from 40% in the preceding two-year span, according to Mr. Bowman's newsletter. The biggest gains in the past three years came from consulting fees, which rose 33%; accounting revenues were up only 14%.

Facing such conditions, Peat, Marwick, Mitchell & Co., the second-biggest firm, has just pushed out or retired 10% of its partners, an unprecedented bloodbath for a major firm.

'I Had to Get Out'

"My boss doubled my quota [for new business] overnight," says a 50-year-old former Peat Marwick partner in the Midwest. "He made it virtually impossible for me to serve my current clients. I had to get out."

Two years ago David J. Charles, now 49, was asked to leave the Miami office of Alexander Grant & Co. after 14 years with the 10th-largest firm. "I was told I wasn't marketing-oriented enough," says Mr. Charles, who now has his own practice. "I'm glad to be out of the big-firm rat race."

As competition to audit big public companies heats up, major accounting firms are trying to expand by acquiring smaller firms. Arthur Young & Co., the sixth-biggest firm, began doing business in Arkansas through an acquisition, and Coopers & Lybrand (No. 3) and Peat Marwick have sharply increased their Florida business that way.

Some small firms say they must merge to survive. In Tallahassee, Fla., May, Zima & Co. says it sent a "prospectus" profiling its business to eight major firms hoping that one will make an offer. "Our revenues have flattened over the past year and we just can't compete with the big firms' financial and marketing resources," says John P. Thomas, May Zima's managing partner.

Big firms also are hiring sales specialists from other fields. Peat Marwick's William Goldberg, a former marketer of financial services for Continental Illinois National Bank & Trust Co., says that "peripheral services" around the audit can be used as a "marketing tool" to expand business.

Mr. Goldberg recently offered to review the tax returns of the top officers of United Bankers of Waco, Texas, a nine-bank holding company, for possible conflict-of-interest problems. "It's a great idea," says Matt Landry, United Bankers president. "And it fits in with a new ethics policy we're drafting." He notes that Peat Marwick is charging only $100 to $200 per review.

But Jim Ainsworth, managing partner of Ainsworth & Lambert, a small firm in Commerce, Texas, isn't happy. Ainsworth & Lambert lost the auditing business of First National Bank of Commerce to Peat Marwick after the bank was acquired by United Bankers. However, Ainsworth & Lambert continues to do the tax returns of First National's top officers.

"Peat's has been pelting us with senseless questions about the tax returns that have nothing to do with conflict of interest," says Mr. Ainsworth. "It's simply a ploy to take all of First National's business away from us by trying to show we're incompetent."

Service Prompts Switch

Pettibone Corp., a Chicago-based maker of materials-handling equipment, recently switched to Arthur Andersen & Co., the biggest U.S. accounting firm, from Alexander Grant & Co., because of one of Andersen's consulting services. Grant had been Pettibone's auditor for 40 years.

"Andersen not only dropped our fee by 40% but helped us cut machine-tool set-up time at our biggest Chicago plant by up to 50%," says Roger Palmer, a Pettibone vice president. Pettibone has been suffering major losses over the past two years because of increased competition in its industry, and the production-time savings are "happy news," Mr. Palmer says.

Over the past five years, Andersen has hired more than 600 engineers to complement its more than 1,000 accounting partners. "They're a big help in gaining an audit client," says William Hinkel, the Andersen partner in charge of the Pettibone audit. Mr. Hinkel says the plant study was part of Pettibone's audit package and "wasn't billed for separately."

Accounting executives insist that consulting improves the audit's quality. "It helps us know more about our clients," says William Gladstone, the chairman of Arthur Young. And Duane Kullberg, managing partner of Arthur Andersen, says consulting by firms is an "added dimension" that can only spur business and the economy. "The public is the winner, not the loser," he says.

'Law of the Jungle'

But Eli Mason, managing partner of Mason & Co., says increased aggressiveness by big firms trying to lure away small firms' clients has brought "the law of the jungle to what once was a gentleman's profession; only the predators will survive."

Mr. Mason, who also is the chairman of the National Conference of CPA Practitioners, an organization of more than 1,000 small firms, recently complained to New York state regulators that Seidman & Seidman, the 12th-biggest firm in the country, was using false advertising to win clients from small competitors. He cited a Seidman advertisement in the Westchester Business Journal last May 7, aimed at businessmen, that said small firms were "limited in their expertise and you've probably outgrown them already."

Seidman & Seidman says it will fight the charges. If the state finds a violation of professional rules, it can censure, fine, suspend or expel a firm.

Denials and Pride

Big firms deny they are trying to push small ones out of business. But they speak with pride of beefed-up marketing efforts for clients of all sizes. Coopers & Lybrand has doubled the size of its marketing department to 80 people in the past five years. It has been using Yankelovich, Skelly & White, a market-research firm, to query businessmen about such areas as planning for future growth and joint ventures.

"We want to project an image of knowing the businessman's problems so he will associate Coopers & Lybrand with solutions," says James Lafond, the accounting firm's national director of business development.

In the past year and a half, Arthur Young has hired marketers from Uniroyal Inc., the tire maker; Clairol Inc., the hair-products company, and Thomas J. Lipton Inc., the tea concern. "We're educating CPAs on how to close a sale for professional services slowly rather than using the hard sell," says Kenneth J. Wright, Arthur Young's director of marketing development. "Professional marketers are helping us learn how to sell our entire product line, using market research, demographics, positioning and other innovations."

Madison Avenue

"The CPA, once versed only in double-entry bookkeeping, is adding the lexicon of Madison Avenue to his spiel," says Bruce Marcus, a former marketer for Arthur Young and Coopers & Lybrand who has just written a book on how to sell professional services.

Consulting has grown so varied that an accountant may be unaware of all the services at his own firm. That's why KMG Main Hurdman last June ran a two-day "trade fair" in Dallas for 500 partners to show them its complete line of 27 "products," including pension consulting, cost-sale analysis for auto dealers and litigation support.

"The partners were so enthusiastic about the chance to learn everything we now offer that we're thinking of using videotapes of the fair as a marketing tool aimed at attracting new clients," says Sam Marks, the firm's marketing consultant. "We want to go out there and really do a selling job so potential clients will come flocking to us."

Says Donald Aronson, Arthur Young's director of marketing:

"Marketing is the new name of the game. The white gloves are off."

Peat Marwick and KMG Main Hurdman Are Holding Preliminary Merger Talks

By Lee Berton
Staff Reporter of The Wall Street Journal

NEW YORK—Peat, Marwick, Mitchell & Co., the second-biggest U.S. accounting firm, and KMG Main Hurdman, the ninth-largest, are holding preliminary merger talks, officials at both firms said.

The officials stressed that no formal merger agreements had been signed. But one noted that data had been exchanged on revenue per partner and per country and on capital adequacy.

If the firms merge, the combination would produce the biggest U.S. and world accounting organizations, displacing Chicago-based Arthur Andersen & Co. as No. 1. World-wide, Andersen has annual revenue of about $1.6 billion, while a merged Peat-KMG would come close to $2.5 billion.

Duane Kullburg, managing partner and chief executive of Arthur Andersen, noted that "competitive pressures are pushing" all major accounting firms to consider the possibility of merging. "The hurdles of combining two big firms' cultures are great, but if two that fit could do it they could reap benefits beyond size alone," he said.

Arthur Bowman, editor of the Public Accounting Report, an Atlanta newsletter, noted that 68% of Peat's world-wide revenue is from U.S. operations, while only 23% of KMG Main Hurdman's revenue comes from the U.S. "Size is a big attraction to audit clients these days, but these two firms also seem to mesh well in strengths and weaknesses," Mr. Bowman said.

Last year, Price Waterhouse, the fifth-biggest U.S. accounting firm, and Deloitte, Haskins & Sells, the seventh-biggest, explored a possible merger that also would have produced the world's largest accounting firm. But failure to obtain partners' approval in Britain scotched the effort.

Numerous Mergers

Mr. Bowman noted that during the past three years the eight biggest U.S. accounting firms have merged with 50 smaller accounting firms, while the next eight biggest have had 100 mergers. "Pressure from clients to reduce fees is high and it takes from five to eight years for

*Wall St J, Sept, 23, 1985

the big accounting firms to groom productive partners, who they may easily lose to industry," he said. "The merger route may be the answer."

Stanley R. Klion, executive vice chairman of Peat Marwick International, the world-wide organization that includes Peat's U.S. operations, said Peat has discussed merger possibilities with several accounting firms during the past few months. "But we wouldn't merge for size alone, because we believe we have sufficient resources for growth and to maintain our professional needs," he added.

Sam Marks, a KMG Main Hurdman spokesman, said, "We've been approached by six major accounting firms over the past twelve months. We haven't entered into formal negotiations with any of them."

Other officials at both firms, who requested anonymity, confirmed that Peat and KMG Main Hurdman are holding informal merger discussions. But they noted that the talks are "very preliminary, and could easily go up in smoke in the near future."

Merger Called Difficult

Officials at other accounting firms noted that merging Peat and KMG Main Hurdman would be difficult because Peat has just pushed out or retired 10% of its partners, while KMG Main Hurdman has one of the highest proportions of partners to professional staff of major firms.

Peat now has 7.5 professional staff members for each partner, while KMG Main Hurdman has six professionals for each partner. Most other Big Eight accounting firms have about eight professionals for each partner, while Arthur Andersen and Price Waterhouse have more than 10 for each partner. The fewer professionals per partner, the higher the firm's management costs, and "this could be a difficult hurdle to overcome in this proposed merger for KMG Main Hurdman partners worried about their jobs," said newsletter editor Mr. Bowman.

For the fiscal year ended June 30, Peat had world-wide revenue of more than $1.45 billion, close to $1 billion of which was generated in the U.S. in the year ended March 31, KMG Main Hurdman had revenue of more than $1 billion, of which $234 million came from U.S. operations.

KMG Main Hurdman's Merger Interest May Portend a Marriage of Necessity

By LEE BERTON

Staff Reporter of THE WALL STREET JOURNAL

NEW YORK—KMG Main Hurdman, the current apple of Peat, Marwick, Mitchell & Co.'s eye, is no stranger to the merger mania that has been sweeping the accounting profession the past year.

The two companies are in preliminary discussions for a combination that would produce the biggest accounting firm in the world. KMG Main Hurdman is the ninth-largest U.S. accounting firm; Peat is the second-largest.

But accounting profession officials note that KMG Main Hurdman has been discussing a possible merger with every major accounting firm except Arthur Young & Co. and Price Waterhouse over the past year. And they say that a marriage for KMG Main Hurdman may be more a necessity than a convenience.

'U.S. Clout' an Issue

"KMG Main Hurdman must boost its U.S. marketing clout or it could be left in the lurch as competition continues to increase among major U.S. accounting firms," said James C. Emerson, publisher of the Big Eight Review, an accounting newsletter based in Bellevue, Wash.

While all eight major firms generate at least half their revenue in the U.S., KMG Main Hurdman's international organization, Klynveld Main Goerdeler, based in the Netherlands, gets only 23% of its revenue here.

Also, while KMG Main Hurdman's U.S. revenue rose 19% to $234 million in the year ended March 31, the U.S. revenue of Philadelphia-based Laventhol & Horwath, the 11th-biggest U.S. accounting firm, spurted 31% to $200 million in the year ended Jan. 31. "There is no question that Laventhol is giving Main Hurdman a close race for its money and could be beating it out for business in the U.S.," said the managing partner of another major accounting firm.

Firm Disagrees

Campbell E. Corfe, director of international services of KMG Main Hurdman, disputes this analysis. "We're growing very rapidly in the U.S., with some of our strengths in health care, government service

---

*Wall St J, Sept 24, 1985, at __.

and small business," he says. He notes that over the past two months the firm has gained as clients Healthtext Inc., Raymond International Inc., Ronson Co. and New York City.

"We have extremely strong marketing position in some of the Midwest and Mid-Atlantic states," he adds.

But officials at other U.S. accounting firms say that top executives of Klynveld Main Goerdeler in Europe are unhappy that KMG Main Hurdman doesn't have a stronger U.S. marketing position.

Peat's U.S. Revenue

Of Peat's more than $1.45 billion in revenue for the year ended last June 30, 68% came from U.S. operations.

KMG Main Hurdman is familiar with growth by merger. In 1979, it was formed by a merger of Hurdman & Cranstoun and Main Lafrentz, two much smaller firms with strong accounting and auditing practices. In early 1983, KMG Main Hurdman considered merging with Chicago-based Alexander Grant & Co., the 10th-biggest U.S. accounting firm, but the project fell through.

Mr. Emerson, the newsletter publisher, notes that Peat also is under pressure to increase its overseas business. Only last month Chicago-based Arthur Andersen & Co., the biggest U.S. accounting firm, merged with SGV Group, the biggest Asian accounting cooperative. And other major accounting firms, such as Coopers & Lybrand, third-biggest U.S. firm, and Deloitte Haskins & Sells, the seventh-biggest, are pushing hard to expand business in Asia.

'Enormous Synergy' Seen

Officials at Peat and KMG Main Hurdman privately assert that if the merger goes through, the two firms could, as one partner puts it, "develop enormous synergy because their personnel and resource needs mesh well."

Peat, for example, has only about 1,600 employees in Europe while KMG has more than 12,000. Peat has a bit more than 2,000 in the Far East, where KMG Main Hurdman has double that. But in North America, Peat has more than 16,000 employees while KMG has close to 6,500.

Peat has been trying to shore up its resources in Asia, and recently merged with San Kyung, a major South Korean company, making it the No. 2 firm in revenue there, behind Coopers & Lybrand.

"Business development for major accounting firms is rapidly moving from a national to a global outlook," says KMG Main Hurman's Mr. Corfe. "With all our clientele becoming more multinational, we have to deliver our services across many national boundaries."

Peat Marwick and KMG Main Hurdman Terminate Exploratory Merger Talks

By LEE BERTON
Staff Reporter of THE WALL STREET JOURNAL

NEW YORK—Peat, Marwick, Mitchell & Co. and KMG Main Hurdman said they have called off exploratory merger talks that could have produced the world's largest accounting firm.

In Amsterdam, the Netherlands, John A. Thompson, KMG Main Hurdman chairman, and Larry Horner, Peat Marwick chairman, disclosed that the two organizations had ended merger talks. "The complexities involved" scuttled the plan, they said. Officials of the two firms had been meeting in Amsterdam, where Klynveld Main Goerdeler, KMG's international organization, is based.

Raft of Complex Issues

The two companies apparently couldn't resolve a raft of complex issues that included how to structure the new firm, persons familiar with the talks said.

Peat Marwick is the second largest accounting firm in the U.S.; KMG Main Hurdman ranks ninth in size.

An official of KMG Main Hurdman said the divisive issues included post-merger management structure and how the partnership arrangements of the two firms would have been meshed. "We just felt there were too many issues that couldn't be resolved," the official said. "The complexities are enormous."

While the talks in Amsterdam began early this week, it is understood that informal, preliminary contacts between the two firms were made several months ago.

The failure to reach an agreement illustrates how difficult it is to effect a merger between large accounting firms, where power rests with individual partners. Last year Price Waterhouse, the fifth largest U.S. accounting firm, and Deloitte, Haskins & Sells, seventh biggest, held unsuccessful talks on a merger that would have produced the world's largest accounting organization, eclipsing Chicago-based Arthur Andersen & Co., which has annual revenue of about $1.6 billion worldwide. That effort failed after partners in Britain voted it down.

---

*Wall St J, Sept 25, 1985, at __.

Operations Were Complementary

Revenue of a merged KMG-Peat Marwick would have approached $2.5 billion, with Peat Marwick accounting for almost $1.5 billion.

Officials of the two firms said a major reason they began talking is that the two operations were complementary and didn't overlap much. Of KMG's world-wide revenue, only 23% is generated in the U.S. Peat's U.S. operations account for 68% of its world-wide revenue.

Top executives at other accounting firms said that this second failed attempt at a merger of major firms could put a damper on merger talks among big firms. But they concede that increasing competition among the Big Eight and second-tier firms are forcing all accounting firms to seek mergers with smaller, regional operations. In the past three years, 50 smaller accounting firms have been absorbed by the eight biggest. The second-largest eight firms have had 100 mergers with smaller concerns during the same period.

KMG is known to have discussed a merger with five other firms besides Peat Marwick over the past year.

ITT Moves to Curb Use of Pension Funds By Hostile Acquirer

By a WALL STREET JOURNAL Staff Reporter

NEW YORK—ITT Corp. said its board took steps to protect the company's pension fund assets in the event of a hostile takeover attempt.

In a filing with the Securities and Exchange Commission, ITT said the change would restrict use of excess assets in the retirement plan for salaried employees to funding of obligations to provide post-retirement medical benefits to beneficiaries.

Only after satisfying those obligations could the funds be used for other corporate purposes, the filing said.

A number of companies in recent months have taken similar steps, designed to make it more difficult for a hostile acquirer to use excess assets in benefit plans to help finance debt in a takeover.

ITT's board previously changed a number of the company's bylaws to make a takeover harder. For example, the board made it more difficult for shareholders to call a special meeting.

ITT said the action on its pension fund was taken at a Sept. 10 board meeting and is effective immediately.

"We feel this action is in the best interest of the company," said Rand V. Araskog, ITT's chairman and chief executive officer. Mr. Araskog added that as a result of the changes, any new controlling group won't be able to arbitrarily end the pension plan to raid the excess funds.

But Mr. Araskog emphasized that to the best of ITT's knowledge, no individual, group of individuals or other company is seeking control of ITT.

ITT said that if terminated now, the plan would have just under $100 million in excess funds.

Premerger Considerations

2

The Need for a Firm to Adopt a Merger Policy

In the past, when firms decided they wanted to acquire other firms, they kept it very quiet. It seemed that they made every effort not to disclose their intended purpose. The copy in a 1982 advertisement appearing in Appendix 2-1 was developed by Pannell Kerr Forster. The ad asks, "What's the big secret?" The ad was certainly a good one, strategically. It gave many medium-sized firms, who perhaps did not want to merge with the Big Eight, the opportunity to talk with an excellent firm. I think we will be seeing more ads of this nature in the future.

It is interesting to note that two of the most successful Big Eight firms, Price Waterhouse and Arthur Andersen & Co., have had very little merger activity. It is also interesting to note that you rarely hear about significant numbers of partners leaving those firms. Apparently, the desire to grow internally rather than externally has been the philosophy behind the business plans of these firms for many years. Now, one of these firms has decided to change its philosophy in order to acquire specialty practices—or practices that would enable it to enter a new market. Can the success of these firms perhaps be attributed to their decision *not* to follow the merger route? Are they more successful than those firms that did merge? Is the basic problem whether to merge? While I do not think the answer is yes, the decision not to merge certainly eliminates many of the problems confronting those firms in the course of a merger. **Russ Palmer** proceeded with an extremely active merger plan when he took over the helm of Touche Ross & Co. Touche Ross today is a combination of many good medium-sized firms that existed throughout the country, but its average hourly rate is obviously less than the rate for some of the other Big Eight firms. Touche Ross does not have the large client base that many of the Big Eight have. However, it has a reputation for being able to service the middle market in an excellent fashion.

If a firm decides to go the merger route, it should adopt a formal policy. Obviously, there are many advantages to merging. In an August 1984 article in *Practicing CPA,* [1] Curt Mingle, the managing partner of one of the 25 largest CPA firms, Clifton, Gunderson & Co., indicates that it is essential to provide opportunities for young staff members of the firm and that his firm decided to adopt a merger policy which has been extremely effective. If your firm is discussing an upstream merger, you should be informed of that merger policy. If the merger is the first one for both firms, it is very important to seek an outside counsel, with extensive experience in this area.

When a firm decides it would like to merge, such a decision really should be part of a long-range plan. Today each firm's business plan should include a merger and acquisition philosophy. The enormous investments involved in operating a practice today cause many firms to pursue the upstream merger route. An upstream merger may allow a firm to avoid the tremendous investment in computers and in other areas required to sustain existence and continue growth. Several years ago a CPA firm was equipped merely with calculators, pencils, and labor. Today such organizations are becoming very capital-intensive. Let us now review the main reasons for mergers.

Many firms merge for internal reasons, the major one being poor retirement planning by the firm. Firms often fail to provide for partner retirement. In a 1984 survey of CPA firms considering merging, 80 per cent of the firms surveyed that wanted to sell their practices, merely wanted to be part of another firm's retirement plan. It is quite sad to think of an individual sole practitioner or partners in a medium-sized firm having worked hard all of their lives and then, because of failure to provide for retirement, suddenly having to tear down what they have built. I believe the firms that can institute a funded retirement program today will be the dynamic and active survivors 25 years from now. Also, it is very important for a practitioner who decides to merge to make sure that the other firm is stable. If the only reason for merging is to

---

[1] Mingle, *Making the Marriage Last,* vol 8 no 8 Practicing CPA 1 (Aug 1984).

be included in an unfunded pension, it is critical for the acquiring firm to be a stable one. We will address this issue later on in the handbook.

Another internal reason why firms merge arises out of increases in professional liability premiums per partner. A former partner from J.K. Lasser once told me that partner retirement and insurance issues were the main reasons for the merger with Touche Ross. Thus, another reason why firms are considering merging is to spread the overall insurance cost. When a firm that grosses $1 million pays $5,000 for professional liability insurance and, two years later, has to pay $25,000, assuming a 30 per cent return at the bottom line, it needs to generate an additional $70,000 in business just to cover the cost of the increased insurance premium.

Firms facing lack of management continuity also tend toward mergers. Where there is no successor to take the reins as managing partner, and the firm really has not taken the time to develop any leaders, the result can be a merger. When you consider that CPAs are always advising their clients about various business matters, it is amazing that they do not prepare business plans and cultivate the futures of their own firms. When was the last time you ever heard of a medium-sized firm sending someone to Harvard to attend a six-week managerial program—or the Wharton School or some other fine institution—to further develop management and leadership skills? In one case, a firm in the Northeast with a hundred professionals acquired a small specialty practice and then appointed the partner of that small firm with four personnel as the managing partner of the entire office, simply because the managing partner of the larger office was to retire and there were no partners in his office who demonstrated the desire and possessed the leadership skills to take over the reins.

The need to upgrade level of services is another reason for an upstream merger. Many times a firm will represent a small company that grows into a large company that brings in a signficiant fee. In this situation a merger occurs to provide the services needed to keep the client. It is interesting to note that a local firm in this country with fewer than 30 professionals has been handling one of the largest venture capital companies in the country. This firm has not merged with a larger firm, and, as a result, has lost a tremendous amount of potential work to other firms in the MAS area. This is an excellent firm that has decided not to go the merger route. Incidentally, if your firm is representing a client with a significant billing, this should be a negotiating point at the bargaining table in the merger process.

Potential dissolution is another reason for taking the merger route. If leadership has not been strong within a firm, i.e., if it is floundering and earnings have not kept pace with inflation, then the firm may decide to merge just to save face—both within the community and among the staff. A merger is better than a disastrous breakup.

There are a myriad of external reasons that can motivate a firm to merge or acquire other practices. For example, a firm may decide to merge in order to: complement an existing practice; enter another market in a strategic location; enhance the specialization talent that could be offered to clients; improve overall profitability by eliminating duplicate libraries, office staff, etc. When you consider the marketing efforts, publication requirements, professional staff training, and investment in capital equipment and office systems, a merger can combine many of these expenses and, thereby, significantly improve the bottom line. In other words, economies of scale play a very important role. This is one reason why even the larger firms are merging. Just think of the possibilities that may result from the combination of two large firms. While the process might take about five years to orchestrate, the shakedown period might eliminate approximately 100 different offices, 100 different office managers, duplicate investments and staff training materials, etc. There would also be a significant increase in income per partner through the right combination of firms. Consequently, I think you will see at least one or two combinations of the Big Eight firms in the next two years, either with another Big Eight firm or a second-tier firm.

When a local medium-sized firm does not indicate a need to merge, this normally means that it is doing well, that is to say, it is a growing, profitable, and well-managed firm that sees no reason to change its good profitability and comfort zone. Firms may also discover in the course of merger negotiations that their operating philosophies are dissimilar. When the operating philosophies of each firm are different enough to cause friction, the decision may be not to proceed with the merger. If, for example, a firm with an average net realizable hourly rate of $60 is going to acquire a firm with a $40 average hourly rate, the acquiring firm is going to have problems in raising the rates of the acquiring firms to $60. In order not to turn away clients presently serviced by the acquired firm, the acquired firm may want an agreement that increases will be made over a three-year period. If the acquiring firm wants an immediate substantial increase in fees, the potential loss of clients can be great, and this is not the way a merger will be successful. Perhaps the acquisition should not take place. Additionally, firm philosophies about borrowing money and other issues must be resolved. All too often in a merger there is emphasis on improving the bottom line immediately and not on the streamlining necessary to make the merger successful. Because of this, a merger may get off to a rocky start. Streamlining the merger and team building sessions in the first six months are just as important as improving the bottom line.

The human factor is another reason why firms may decide not to merge. The uncertainty involved in merging often generates staff discomfort which can have a devastating affect on the operation of a new firm. Employees do not know how the new combination will affect their futures and, in turn, the futures of their respective families. They fear how they will fare with a new, younger firm. Will they be promoted, demoted, or have to relocate? Partners in one firm may become managers in the surviving firm. The "shockwaves" of a merger may, in short, be counterproductive to its purpose. Preliminary discussions may alert a firm to these problems.

Deciding on a name for the new firm is another interesting reason why some firms decide not to merge. It is unbelievable how egos can override important business decisions when the time comes to choose a name for a combined practice. It is ludicrous for the receptionist to greet you with six names when you call a CPA firm. No one in the business world should have to wait that long before being able to ask for the person sought. The truth of the matter is that everyone remembers the first name of most medium-sized CPA firms, and this point should be dealt with in negotiations. If a combined firm is having trouble with the name of the firm, then it is obviously going to have a lot more trouble in the future. Where there are problems in selecting the name of a firm, I would recommend that the firms not merge because of the egos involved. It is a sure sign of future problems when people cannot sit down and immediately offer to give something up—such as inclusion of their name in the firm name. What is more important—firm security, bottom line, future growth, or "your name in the firm?" Some may say all four, but the point is to look at the business opportunity at hand.

Additional administrative work is a reason why many medium-sized firms decide not to merge with a regional or national firm. There is a tremendous amount of administrative pressure and a blizzard of paperwork during the first year of a merger which will cause a partner to become very frustrated. It is a good idea for firms to study the entire process and find out exactly what is required and what type of forms are to be completed, because there is not one medium-sized firm that has merged with a national firm and not experienced "shockwaves" from the effects of all the paperwork required. Each partner should be fully aware of this situation before executing an agreement.

Some firms do not want to merge because they have already been through the merging and de-merging process and are very reluctant to cross that threshold again. Personally, I think this is a big mistake.

It is extremely important that the firm that had to de-merge review exactly what went wrong. While no one really knows what is going to happen during the first two years of a new merger, chances are the firm did not properly plan for the merger. Subsequently, the firm discovered things that it might, for the most part, have found out up front if it had gone through the proper process in evaluating the decision to merge. In a recent seminar, a partner in a prestigious firm was somewhat upset because his firm was working on two different mergers which fell through. It was my opinion that the person was an excellent businessman and, perhaps, made the best decision not to proceed with the merger.

Substantial independence-related issues will arise for those medium-sized firms deciding to merge with a large national firm. For example, after you become a partner with the large firm, you will be presented with a list of all the clients they represent and you will be expected to divest yourself of ownership of those clients. Many times partners must sell stock at a loss or at a substantial profit when in fact they had no intention to do so. There may also be individuals on the staff of the medium-sized CPA firm whose parents or other relatives have important positions with clients. These independence-related issues, in turn, may present problems relating to overall philosophy and policy of the firm. One firm lost two outstanding senior accountants as a result of this very situation. In this case, their relatives were chief financial officers of major corporations, but the acquiring firm had a policy that would not allow a promotion to manager. These are things that no one thinks about normally, but which should be considered in the decision to merge with a larger firm.

Sometimes a medium-sized firm does not want to merge because members feel in doing so they will no longer be able to provide their clients with the same degree of personal service which enabled them to become successful to begin with. There will be more time devoted to recruiting, meetings, and administration which may affect the amount of hours devoted to serving clients. However, on the other hand, the professional in the acquiring firm can assist in providing existing and new services for your clients. A firm being courted for a potential merger cannot afford to be naive about the fact that a larger firm partner brings increased performance pressures and administrative responsibilities.

Potential loss of clients can be another reason for a firm's decision not to merge. It can be devastating for firms that do merge to lose what they have worked for so hard. I fail to understand how any firm could forget that it is the personal attention that matters to a client. In the eyes of certain clients, it is the individual, not necessarily always the firm, that is representing that client, particularly in the small and medium-sized business sector. In a merger, participants may fail to consider that clients have a right to choose who is going to represent them and, thus, it is critical to solidify client relations before and after a merger. There are other reasons for not merging, such as the potential loss of support and professional staff who may decide to leave the firm because of a merger, especially in case of a small family-type firm.

Following are questions and answers about mergers and acquisitions issues.

Questions and Answers

Question: Are you aware of any current litigation arising out of a sale of a CPA practice?

Answer: A suit was recently filed by a CPA firm that sold its practice to another CPA firm where the purchase price was based on subsequent collections from existing clients. The CPA firm that bought the practice started to lose clients, which meant that the seller's *pocketbook* was affected. The seller subsequently sued the buyer for malpractice and the case is now pending in court.

Question: I have an opportunity to take in a partner who is with a large national firm and has expertise in an area that would be excellent for our firm. However, I am afraid of the covenant not to compete agreement in his firm's partnership agreement. Should I approach this person and consummate an agreement to have him come with us?

Answer: This is basically a business judgment and the decision depends on whether you are prepared to be sued by the firm for enticing the individual to break his covenant. Obviously, the best approach would be to sit down with the firm and to work out an agreement whereby the individual withdraws from the firm and a value is determined and paid for any clients that he would take. This particular agreement should be made between the partner leaving the firm and the firm, and should not include your firm at all. If the firm is unwilling to settle, then you have to be prepared to be sued and it is probably not worth it. When a CPA firm decides to admit a partner that has left another firm, it is extremely important to be sure that particular partner has resolved all differences and has bought out his or her contract. You do not want to inherit anyone else's problems because they will always haunt you.

Question: What is the normal period covered by a covenant not to compete agreement in a merger with a large national firm?

Answer: It is generally at least three years to a maximum of five years.

Question: Are there any hidden tax considerations?

Answer: There are generally none, unless you decide to join a large national firm and leave via the de-merger agreement. The return of your capital investment may be ordinary income. You should investigate this issue before merging.

Question: What about back professional liability insurance premiums? What is the procedure?

Answer: Generally, a firm that is acquired must take out a five-year back professional liability insurance policy. The cost is normally 100 to 150 per cent of one year's premium. This amount is generally paid by the acquired firm. However, in view of recent substantial increases in professional liability insurance premiums, the issue of who pays the premium should be negotiated.

Question: Should an outside consultant be hired to evaluate the merger?

Answer: Yes. Before merging or acquiring a practice, an outside consultant who has had years of experience in the CPA profession should be retained to provide assistance in the merger process.

Question: Our firm would like to acquire another firm but we have no signed partnership agreement. Can we proceed without one?

Answer: This has been known to happen but it does not make good business sense. It is extremely important for your firm to finalize the agreement before an acquisition. Sometimes, partners have difficulty with a few provisions in an agreement, and, in order to have the agreement executed, it may be necessary to grandfather certain issues, such as a covenant not to compete.

If necessary, the firm should engage a facilitator to assist in finalizing the agreement.

Question: In a merger, how important is the adoption of an overall firm philosophy?

Answer: Very important. If firm A has always borrowed on its receivables and firm B has never borrowed except for the purchase of capital equipment, then there may be a problem. Therefore, before the merger agreement is signed, a firm philosophy should be adopted for the critical issues. For example, providing funding for the future growth of the combined firm should be discussed. It is very important to prepare accurate financial projections to demonstrate that there may be a need to borrow and adopt a firm philosophy on this issue beforehand (*some partners do not like debt*).

Question: Should one-, three-, or five-year projections be prepared for an acquisition?

Answer: Before each acquisition is finalized, it is very important to prepare at least three-year projections for the combined firms. Using Lotus or some other software, you can build a myriad of assumptions (worst case versus best case scenario) to identify potential problems such as effect of retiring partners, admission of new partners, pay-back of acquisition, office space needs, increase in professional liability insurance, etc.

Question: Should a merger/acquisition policy be included in a firm's business plan?

Answer: Yes. Following is a list of the items that should be included in a firm's business plan:

1. Financial Projection: Three-Year
2. Mergers and Acquisitions Plan
3. Marketing Plan
4. Professional Productivity Plan
5. Partner In-Training Plan
6. Computer Efficiency Program
7. Analysis of Firm Profitability
8. Growth—Other Offices
9. Professional Development Goals
10. Client Retention Program
11. Strategic Goals
12. Quality Control for All Departments
13. Professional Liability Insurance
14. Associations of CPA Firms
15. Firm Administrator
16. Retirement Program
17. Partnership Agreement Update
18. Facilities and Equipment Program
19. Mission Statement for Firm
20. Paraprofessional Program
21. Staff Utilization Review
22. Management Advisory Service Department
23. Entrepreneur Services Program

24. Training Programs—Support Staff
25. Partner Team Building Program
26. Turnover—Closing the Revolving Door
27. Compensation—Partners
28. Product Sales
29. Firm Advisory Board
30. Recruiting Program

Question: If I have a five-partner firm with a volume of $1.5 million, would I be an attractive candidate for an upstream merger with a large national firm?

Answer: Generally no, because the volume per partner is low. Sometimes a merger might occur if only two partners were admitted and three of the partners in the firm became managers in the acquiring firm. If this is the case, then you must be very careful because the three managers could control a significant volume and could leave the firm to start their own practice, which would result in the merger not being a success.

Question: If I have a $2 million dollar firm, and I would like to acquire a sole practitioner's practice with a volume of $.4 million and 10 people, what should the initial step be?

Answer: First of all, if people have been on their own for a long time, merger would mean they would have to curb their egos. One of the best ways to determine whether there is a potential conflict between partners is to take personality profiles of the sole practitioner and the partners of the acquiring firm's office to determine the existence of any potential conflicts. This is presently being done by several major corporations and firms, and the results often reveal significant problem areas. In all mergers, where possible, I would recommend utilization of these tests so that new colleagues will know how to deal with each other in a more effective manner. (See Chapter 6.)

Question: What should be the general time frame for a merger?

Answer: It has always amazed me that we generally date our spouses for quite some time before we get married. However, businessmen and women decide over dinner that a merger should occur between firms. In other words, it does not make much sense to make an important and sometimes irrevocable decision on short notice. It is extremely important that partners from both firms spend a considerable amount of time getting to know each other and determine whether there is a shared value of philosophies. I recommend that a merger take at least six months to set up.

Question: Should a new partner who is admitted to your firm pay for the goodwill of the firm?

Answer: This is a question frequently asked by many practitioners, particularly partners in medium-sized firms. Some national firms require a newly admitted partner to pay a certain amount for the goodwill applicable to each unit that is received. Some other national firms do not charge for the good will factor when a person is admitted to the firm via merger. Following is an example of a proposed formula for admitting a new partner to a medium-sized firm:

Proposed Formula for Admitting New Partner

1.	Gross firm billing	$2,500,000
2.	Factor—good will	75%
3.	Total	$1,875,000
4.	Divided by number of shares	100
5.	Value per share	$18,750
6.	Shares for new partner	2.5[2]
7.	Purchase price	$46,875
8.	Payment term	7 years[3]
9.	Interest	10%
10.	Annual payment	$9,338.52
11.	Annual distribution	$12,000 [4]

Question: If I am acquiring a practice with a substantial portion of the firm's revenue derived from personal financial planning, is there any issue I should be aware of before consummating the merger.

Answer: Yes, you should ascertain beforehand whether the firm should have been registered under the Investment Advisers Act of 1940. If it should have been, you may be inheriting future lawsuits. You should discuss this matter with legal counsel and your professional liability insurance carrier.

---

[2] Initial purchase of 2.5, right to purchase an additional 7.5 shares during the next five years.

[3] New partner purchases interest from existing partner and payment is made over a seven-year period.

[4] First distribution of profits after salaries and interest on capital is made to new partners so that they can pay off their note.

Question: If your CPA firm is in jeopardy, how can you tell if you are headed for a potential divorce?

Answer: Lack of communication among the partners is the first sign. When a marriage fails, it can generally be attributed to the fact that no one really wants to talk about issues anymore and parties decide to go their separate ways. In a CPA firm, the same scenario exists when each partner, in effect, becomes a sole practitioner within the firm. They don't communicate with each other. Unfortunately, many firms continue to operate in this manner, and, eventually, they dissolve. Sometimes, nepotism may cause disenchantment and jealousy which may lead to partners leaving the firm. Again, there may be cliques and communication problems. Finally you may be aware of bad blood, for example, partners that started the firm together may change during a lifetime, and end up in divorce. In other words, they didn't grow together and developed different philosophies. They argue about everything. It takes a very strong leader in today's environment to keep a firm on the right path. The leader must also be alert for signs of trouble.

Question: A partner of a large regional CPA firm was asked the following question: What percentage of the mergers consummated by you during the last five years were successful?

Answer: Our firm finalized 12 mergers during that time, with nine satisfactory ones and three that just did not work. The main reason the three did not work was people problems. Our firm did not perform a sufficient study up front to determine the philosophy of the partners of the firm, work habits, etc. It taught us that we must spend a tremendous amount of time up front to make sure that everyone is on the same wave length.

Question: When a firm is on the verge of breaking up, is there any last resort?

Answer: Yes, I would recommend engaging an outside facilitator to conduct a partner retreat for a minimum of two days with confidential questionnaries being executed by all partners and submitted to the facilitator before your retreat. This is a last-ditch effort which should be tried before a firm is dissolved.

Selected Reading List

Coker, *Some Practical Tips on Buying or Merging and Accounting Practice,* 14 Prac Acct 17 (Mar 1981).

Lang, *Buying, Merging or Selling an Accounting Practice,* 16 Prac Acct 87 (Nov 1983).

Liberty, *To Merge or Not to Merge,* 151 J Acct 52 (Jan 1981).

What's the big secret?

Until now, the secret has been merger discussions.

Until now, the secret has been even disclosing a desire to merge.

Just read the JOURNAL classified section. There are dozens of merger opportunities — that is, with box numbers. But mergers are made between people and firms, not post office boxes.

Pannell Kerr Forster is a firm of people looking for a select few merger opportunities. We seek to associate with people and firms of the same calibre who share the same aspirations. We set high standards for ourselves and expect nothing short of these standards from merger candidates.

Our practice philosophy statement clearly emphasizes that we will selectively pursue mergers to

- Develop qualified executives and staff.
- Expand or develop new expertise.
- Gain access to new market areas.
- Increase activity in currently served areas.

In view of the spiraling costs inherent in today's conduct of professional practice, the standards overload, administrative burdens, and identity maintenance; we would be interested in hearing from those of you who share our objectives and would be willing to explore the potential advantages of merger between our organizations.

We believe all mergers should be mutually advantageous and profitable, and after all, we do practice to make profits.

If you are interested in exploring merger opportunities with us, please call or write Charles Kaiser, Jr., Managing Partner, Pannell Kerr Forster, Administrative Office, 262 North Belt East, Suite 300, Houston, Texas 77060, (713) 999-5134 or contact the Partner in Charge of any of our offices.

Now it's no longer a secret. We are interested in talking merger but don't have a box number. Instead we have an address, a phone number, and PEOPLE.

UNITED STATES OFFICES

Alexandria, VA	Hollywood, FL	No. Palm Beach, FL
Atlanta, GA	Honolulu, HI	Orlando, FL
Boca Raton, FL	Houma, LA	Philadelphia, PA
Boston, MA	Houston, TX	Phoenix, AZ
Brentwood, CA	Incline Village, NV	Reno, NV
Chicago, IL	Lewiston, ID	St. Louis, MO
Cleveland, OH	Los Angeles, CA	San Diego, CA
Columbus, OH	Media, PA	San Francisco, CA
Dallas, TX	Memphis, TN	San Juan, PR
Denver, CO	Miami, FL	Sarasota, FL
Detroit, MI	Minneapolis, MN	Seattle, WA
Ft. Lauderdale, FL	Mobile, AL	Spokane, WA
Greensboro, NC	New Orleans, LA	Washington, DC
Hartford, CT	Newport Beach, CA	Wenatchee, WA
	New York, NY	Woodland Hills, CA

PANNELL KERR FORSTER
WORLDWIDE

(Reprinted with permission).

Prospective Merger Questionnaire and Initial Meeting Considerations

3

Once your firm has decided to acquire a practice or merge upstream, certain materials should be prepared. This chapter contains a Prospective Merger Questionnaire which should be completed. There are also a list of considerations that should be addressed during the initial meeting, a marketing program questionnaire that should be completed, and a client acceptance form that should be reviewed.

It is extremely important to address philosophical issues such as firm borrowing and to resolve the name of the firm in advance. Too often, firms decide to address the delicate issues last when they should be discussed during the initial meeting. The first rule is not to waste each other's time and to be very honest about issues.

Robert Liberty, CPA a former managing partner of Moss Adams & Co., refers to three schedules in his article "To Merge or Not to

Merge.''[1] I have included these schedules in this chapter for your review. The first schedule provides a list of objectives for the firm that is to be acquired. The second schedule lists concerns of the merger candidate, and then presents six merger criteria of Moss Adams & Co.

Prospective Merger Questionnaire

If your firm is planning to acquire a practice, it is important to obtain as much data as possible about the firm. The following questionnaire has been designed to incorporate the salient data that would provide partners with the necessary information to proceed with further discussions. When preparing the questionnaire, it is imperative that the acquiring firm review the financial data of the firm to be acquired and attach copies of the financial statement and the most recent tax return to the questionnaire. Finally, it is of paramount importance also to attach a copy of the firm's partnership agreement to this questionnaire.

---

[1] Liberty, *To Merge or Not to Merge*, 151 J Acct 52 (Jan 1981). Copyright © 1981 by American Institute of Certified Public Accountants, Inc. Opinions of the authors are their own and do not necessarily reflect policies of the AICPA.

PROSPECTIVE MERGER QUESTIONNAIRE

I. GENERAL
   A. NAME OF FIRM: _____
   B. ADDRESS: _____
       _____
       _____

   C. TELEPHONE NUMBER: _____
   D. ADDRESSES OF OTHER OFFICES:
       _____
       _____
       _____

   E. Date firm started _____
   F. Gross volume _____
   G. Number of partners _____

        Signed: _____

APPENDIX A

II. PERSONNEL INFORMATION

Name	Age	Years In Public Accounting	Years With Firm	CPA Y/N	Specialization	Education School	Degree	Current Annual Comp	Billing Current	Charge Hours Last Fiscal Year

II.   PERSONNEL INFORMATION (cont.)
    B. Partner's Background of Experience

Partner	Years with Your Firm	Years a Partner	Prior Professional Experience

II.   PERSONNEL INFORMATION (cont.)
    C. Partner's Activities (current and prior) in Professional Societies:

Partner	Professional Society	Office or Committee

    D. If any substantial amount of time is spent regularly by a partner on other than firm business, give name of partner and describe activity:

_____

_____

_____

_____

    E. Have any partners within the past three years left the firm? If so, please provide specifics:

_____

_____

_____

_____

III. Complete *Appendix A* (list of personnel which should include all employees)

IV. *DESCRIPTION OF FIRM*

Attach statement—include history and major events significant to firm's development, client information (e.g., number of publicly held companies, number of clients with nationally known products but not publicly owned), specialty areas of firm, staff evaluation procedures, recruiting program, and fringe benefits provided. This should be self-explanatory.

V. *STATISTICS*

A. Total Personnel for All Offices

	Number	Number of CPAs
Partners:	_____	_____
Professional Staff:	_____	_____
Paraprofessionals	_____	_____
Computer Personnel	_____	_____
Clerical Staff:	_____	_____
Other Personnel:	_____	_____
Total:	_____	_____

B. Breakdown by Office Location

Office Location	No. of Partners	No. of Staff	Other Personnel	Total
_____	_____	____	_____	_____
_____	_____	____	_____	_____
_____	_____	____	_____	_____
_____	_____	____	_____	_____
_____	_____	____	_____	_____

V. STATISTICS (cont.)

C. Annual Fees of ALL Offices:

_____ _____ for Fiscal Year Ending _____
(accrual basis) (cash basis)

D. Amount of Professional Liability Coverage: $_____

E. Name of Insurance Company: _____

_____

F. Expiration Date of Coverage: _____

G. Analysis of Practice:

	Approx. %
Opinion Audit Work:	_____
Compilation & Review:	_____

	No. of Individual
Tax Return Preparation:	_____ Returns Prepared:

Tax Planning: _____

Management Services: _____

Write-up Work: _____

Computer Services: _____

    TOTAL: _____

H. *BILLING DATE:*

   1. Billing Rates:

      _____ per hour - Partners

      _____ per hour - Professional Staff

      _____ per hour - Paraprofessionals

      _____ per hour - Clerical

   2. How are billing rates determined?

    _____

    _____

V. STATISTICS (cont.)

   3. Frequency of billing.

      Method (approximate percentage)

      a. Monthly _____

      b. Quarterly _____

      c. Annually _____

   4. Average Net Realizable Hourly Rate

    _____

    Fiscal Year Ended _____ _____

    Fiscal Year Ended _____ _____

    Fiscal Year Ended _____ _____

I. Financial Data

   Revenue (accrual basis)

   Fiscal year ended _____

   Fiscal year ended _____

   Fiscal year ended _____

   Projected revenues for next twelve months _____

   Range of fees per year (Appendix B) _____

J. Attach name, fee and realization information for ten largest clients (see Appendix C.)

K. Attach name and fee information for clients that have left the firm during the last three years with fees in excess of $5,000.00

L. Fringe benefits — See Appendix E

M. Office or Administrative Manual (attach copy if possible)

N. Client Acceptance Policy (state procedure)

    _____

    _____

———————————————————
———————————————————

O. Monthly newsletter to clients: YES___NO___
    If yes, attach a copy

VI. *CONTINUING PROFESSIONAL EDUCATION*
     Describe firm's educational program. Include data for both
     outside and in-house programs.

———————————————————
———————————————————
———————————————————
———————————————————
———————————————————
———————————————————
———————————————————
———————————————————
———————————————————
———————————————————

VII. *PHYSICAL PLANT AND EQUIPMENT*
      A. Square Footage: ————————————
      B. Computer Equipment: ————————————

      C. Library (description of accounting, tax and MAS services
          subscribed to):

———————————————————
———————————————————
———————————————————
———————————————————
———————————————————

VIII. *REASONS FOR INTEREST IN MERGERS*

———————————————————
———————————————————
———————————————————

IX.   Have charges ever been brought against the firm or any of its
      professional personnel by any governmental agency (including
      the SEC, IRS, State Board of Accountancy), the American Insti-
      tute of CPAs or a state CPA society?_____
      If yes, describe the charges and outcome (attach separate state-
      ment).
      Are the firm or any of its professional personnel presently in-

volved in litigation in which professional competence is questioned?_____

    A. Has there ever been such involvement, or is there reason to believe that there may be such in the near future? _____

    B. If yes, provide details in separate statement.

X.   Bank References:

    1. _____

    2. _____

XI.   Managing Partner:

_____

XII.   List below any affiliations your firm has with foreign accounting firms:

_____

_____

_____

XIII.   Is the firm a present member of an association of CPA firms?
YES__ NO__
If yes, provide details
Name: _____
Years a member: _____
If no, were you ever a member of an association of CPA firms?
YES__ NO__
If yes, provide details.
Name: _____
Years a member _____
Reason for leaving _____
Is a formal quality control document in use?
YES__ NO__

XIV.   Is your firm a member of the AICPA _____?
Private Companies Practice Section _____?
SEC Practice Section _____?
If yes, have you undergone a PCPS or an SECPS peer review under the section (attach copy of recommendations)?
_____?
Date held _____
Scheduled to be held _____
Firm that conducted peer review

_____

_____

XV.   Name of law firm that is representing firm.

_____

XVI.   Describe partner compensation policy.

MERGER DOCUMENT
SCHEDULE OF PERSONNEL

Name
Position
Age
Classification
CPA status
Years in public accounting
Specialization
Education—school
Degree
Current billing rate
Proposed rate
Charge hours—last year
Budget—charge hour—current year

MERGER DOCUMENT
Composition of practice

Number of clients with annual billings of:	Audit	Tax	MAS	Other
50,000				
10,000 to 50,000				
5000 to 10,000				
2,000 to 5,000				
Under 2,000				
Total	≡≡≡	≡≡	≡≡	≡≡≡

By area   Billing
Service hours
Average billing
Per service hour

LIST OF TEN LARGEST CLIENTS

YEAR OBTAINED	CLIENT NAME	CHARGE HOURS	FEE	REALIZATION

CLIENT MIX

Real Estate
Manufacturing
Retail/Wholesale
Service Industry
Professional Firms
Other Business
Healthcare Service

Total   100%

FRINGE BENEFITS

Insurance	Carrier	Coverage	Paid by Firm or Employee
Hospitalization	_____	_____	_____
Health	_____	_____	_____
Disability	_____	_____	_____
Life	_____	_____	_____
Other_____	_____	_____	_____
(specify)			

Disability Policy
  for partners_____
  for employees_____
Death Policy
  for partners_____
  for employees_____
Retirement Policy
  for partners_____
  for employees_____

	Paid by Firm or Employee
CPA EXAMINATION FEES	_____
STATE CPA SOCIETY DUES	_____
AICPA DUES	_____

Initial Meeting Considerations

I.   DETERMINE MERGER OBJECTIVES

    A.   Maintain the *partner*-shared values of quality service and challenging and rewarding careers

    B.   Provide *reasonable* assurance that the partners and employees from both firms will have the opportunity to have rewarding careers with the combined firm

    C.   A merger of *relative equals* can provide reasonable assurance that a substantial majority of people from both organizations will have rewarding careers with the combined firm

II. INITIAL MEETING CONSIDERATIONS

    A.   Major points

        1.   Identify partners from both firms that are best suited to direct the merger discussion

        2.   Explore the name change

           a.   Sensitive

           b.   Greatest obstacle to overcome

        3.   Identify managing partner

        4.   Identify department heads

           a.   Forget co-department heads

        5.   Draft office layout

        6.   Draft document

           a.   Capital contribution

           b.   Ownership

           c.   Covenants not to compete

        7.   Explore the worst scenario (de-merger agreement?)

        8.   Guarantee each respective partner's income

           a.   Determine average partners' earning

        9.   Review retirement and benefit programs

      10. Obtain information about average hourly rate—net fees

      11. Tax considerations

      12. Current litigation

      13. Client retention problems

          a.   Discuss beforehand with major clients

          b.   Identify the clients that may object

          c.   Guarantee fees and charges not to exceed previous years

          d.   Guarantee the same professional staff will serve on the engagement

          e.   Chance—one year to perform under new umbrella

      14. Practical considerations

          a.   The unavoidable facts that people will leave and conditions will change

          b.   If you have good staff and managers they may be assigned to newer or more profitable clients—thus disrupting part of the practice

    15.   Review firm's marketing program

Review of Marketing Program

To assist a firm that is interested in acquiring another practice, you should review its marketing capabilities. The following is a marketing questionnaire that can be completed to determine the strength of a firm's marketing program. If the majority of the answers are "no," then, as the acquiring firm, you must realize that it will require a great deal of time to enhance the marketing skills of professionals in the acquired firm. If a majority of the answers are "yes," then, as the acquiring firm, you will probably benefit significantly from their marketing capabilities.

Marketing Program

Questionnaire for CPA Firms

		YES	NO
1.	Does your firm have a formal and organized marketing plan?	——	——
2.	Does your firm have a marketing coordinator (not a CPA)?	——	——
3.	Does your firm have someone monitor the newspaper about present clients or potential business?	——	——
4.	Does your firm have a brochure?	——	——
5.	Does your firm have an outside marketing consultant or public relations firm?	——	——
6.	Does your firm have a logo?	——	——
7.	Does your firm have a monthly client newsletter?	——	——
8.	Does your firm conduct quarterly seminars for clients and nonclients?	——	——
9.	Does your firm have impressive office facilities?	——	——
10.	Does your firm have an excellent receptionist?	——	——
11.	Have your secretaries received training on improving their telephone services?	——	——
12.	Does your firm conduct monthly management meetings for cross-selling firm services?	——	——
13.	Does your firm have a program for partners and managers to write articles for publications?	——	——
14.	Is your firm a member of the local chamber of commerce?	——	——
15.	Does your firm have a charitable contribution program?	——	——
16.	Does your firm have a quarterly or semiannual meeting with each client and its banker, insurance agent, and attorney?	——	——
17.	Has your firm targeted any potential clients and developed a plan of action?	——	——
18.	Has your firm developed a needs assessment questionnaire for your present and prospective clients?	——	——

		YES	*NO*
19.	Have your firm's management group members received training to improve their presentation skills and proposal content?	——	——
20.	Does your firm have a good relationship with the print media?	——	——
21.	Does your firm have an advertising program?	——	——
22.	Does your firm have a specialty, such as health care, financial planning, etc., that you promote?	——	——
23.	Does your firm utilize Ashton-Tate's dBase III programs to market professional services?	——	——
24.	Does your firm have a working relationship with some other regional or national CPA firm?	——	——
25.	Does your firm issue a monthly marketing calendar for the management team (*calendar* would include speaking engagements and any other practice development activities)?	——	——
26.	Does your firm have a community visibility program?	——	——
27.	Does your firm monitor the competition and know their strengths and weaknesses?	——	——
28.	Has your firm considered acquiring a local practice with a unique specialty?	——	——
29.	Has your firm considered opening a new office?	——	——
30.	Does your firm have an excellent support staff?	——	——

Review of Client Acceptance

Because of increases in professional liability insurance costs, it is very important to review the client acceptance policy of the firm being acquired. Following is a client acceptance form which can be used to review the adequacy of a firm's policies.

Additionally, it is extremely important to determine whether investment tax advice has been rendered during the past five years, particularly in investments that did not make economic sense. Several cases are presently pending in court, and, if the Internal Revenue Service wins, there will be many investors who will probably sue their advisors, including CPAs.

In 1983, an acquired firm could purchase a five-year professional liability tail policy which was 150 per cent of one year's premium. Today, it may be possible to purchase a *one-year* tail policy at 200 per cent of one year's premium. Thus, it is extremely important for the acquiring firm to receive a letter from the insurance carrier indicating that back liability insurance has been obtained. This important issue is to make sure that the acquiring firm reviews the quality control and client acceptance policies of the merged firm.

Client Acceptance Report*

Although we have an active Practice Development Committee, and we are interested in obtaining new clients, it is extremely important to obtain as much data as possible about a prospective new client. Therefore, the firm has developed this Client Acceptance Report which will determine whether the firm will represent the client. Certain information will be included in our data base for practice management purposes.

This report is to be completed for every potential client of the firm. All information must be completed by a manager and submitted to a partner for review. The report, together with any additional data, must be submitted to the Client Acceptance Committee.

1.   Client name _____
2.   Client address _____
     _____
     _____

* This form was developed by R.J. Gallagher & Associates, Inc. for CPA firms.

3.   Nature of business _____

      _____
      _____

4.   Client contact _____
      Position _____
5.   Owner of company _____
6.   Law firm _____
      Primary banker _____
      Other bank _____
      Insurance agent _____
7.   Previous CPA firm _____
      A. Length of service _____ (years)
      B. Annual fees _____
      C. Billed - paid____yes ____no*
      D. Partner in charge of client _____

      _____
      *If no, why and how much is still outstanding?

8.   When was the last time the client changed CPA firms?
      _____
      Name of previous CPA firm and, if possible, give reason for
      changing_____

      _____
      _____

9.   If a business client, please provide the following information:

	Year to date*	Last year
sales		
net income (loss)		
current ratio		
net worth		
bank debit		

      *State period covered _____
10.   Does the client expect to borrow additional monies?
      ____yes ____no
      Attach information
11.   What is the nature of our engagement? _____
      _____
      _____

		DUE DATE
A. audit	___	_____
B. compilation	___	_____
C. review	___	_____

D. corporate tax return   _____   _____
E. pension work   _____   _____
F. personal tax returns   _____   _____
G. personal financial planning   _____   _____
H. write-up services   _____   _____
I. other _____   _____   _____

12. If a financial statement is to be prepared, who will review the statement?
     A. client board
     B. banker
     C. client's law firm
     D. bonding company
     E. other _____

13. Company officer's name:
     A. name _____
        address _____
        _____

     B. name _____
        address _____
        _____

     C. name _____
        address _____
        _____

     D. name _____
        address _____
        _____

14. Will we prepare the personal tax return for the owners?
     _____yes _____no
     If yes, please indicate that you have reviewed last year's personal return and list any unusual items in the return:
     _____
     _____
     _____
     _____

15. If closely held, have any judgments or liens been recorded against the owners?
     Have any of the shareholders or officers declared bankruptcy?_____yes _____no
     If so, state name _____
     Date _____

16. What is our fee estimate? _____

17. What is the anticipated realization? _____

18. What is the time period when the work will be performed?

19. Please indicate the names of the partners and professional staff who have met the prospect

_____

_____

20. How did they hear of our firm (give name)?
     A. another client _____
     B. bank _____
     C. insurance agent _____
     D. attorney _____
     E. other _____

21. What is the current status of the client's payables?
     current   _____
     30-60   _____
     61-90   _____
     over 90 days   _____

22. When were bills from the previous CPA firm paid?
     30-60   _____
     60-90   _____
     over 90 days   _____

23. Are there opportunities for the firm to perform additional services?

24. Is the client involved in any current litigation?
     _____yes   _____no
     If so, please state briefly the nature of the suit:

_____

_____

_____

_____

25. Have all previous corporate returns been filed and taxes paid?
     _____yes   _____no

26. Who is the officer responsible for the financial operation of the company?
     name _____
     title _____
     years with company _____

27. Did the previous auditors prepare a management letter?
     _____yes   _____no
     If so, attach a copy of the latest letter to this report.

28. What is the general condition of the accounting records?
    excellent _____
    good   _____
    average   _____
    poor   _____
    If the records are poor, please state how many adjusting entries were made by the previous auditor.
    _____

29. Does the person responsible for the day-to-day financial operation of the company have adequate background and experience?
    ____yes ____no

30. Is there any reason why the firm should not accept this client?
    ____yes ____no
    If yes, please comment: _____
    _____
    _____
    _____

31. Is there any independence problem in servicing this client?
    ____yes ____no
    If yes, please comment: _____
    _____
    _____
    _____

32. Should a retainer be requested?
    ____yes ____no
    If so, how much? _____

33. Do we know the industry and have we represented companies in the same industry?
    ____yes ____no
    If not, why should we accept this engagement?
    _____

34. Is this a high-risk engagement?
    ____yes ____no

                              Client approved

                    _____
                    _____
                    _____

Note: Attach a copy of the latest financial statement and a copy of a financial statement for the preceding three years.

OBJECTIVES OF MERGER CANDIDATE:
A CHECKLIST[2]

		Great Significance	Some Significance	No Significance
1.	To secure specialists in audit, tax, Securities and Exchange Commission or management advisory services.			
2.	To secure industry specialists.			
3.	To participate in training programs.			
4.	To participate in recruiting programs.			
5.	To obtain benefit of quality control procedures.			
6.	To obtain benefit of practice development program.			
7.	As a means to escape from the administrative work involved in a practice and provide more time for client activities and practice development.			
8.	As a means to further specialization on the part of one or more partners.			
9.	To provide additional time to be with family.			
10.	To avoid loss of key clients.			
11.	To secure early retirement for one or more partners.			
12.	To acquire security of a larger organization in the event of illness or lengthy disability.			
13.	As a means to assure payment for interest of older partners and/or payment of retirement programs.			
14.	As a means to ultimately sell the practice.			

[2] *Id.*

	Great Significance	Some Significance	No Significance
15. To be large enough to serve the needs of larger clients through an increase in range of services.			
16. To obtain representation in areas of the country or the world in which present clients now operate.			
17. To improve current income.			
18. To increase retirement benefits.			
19. To provide additional opportunities for staff.			
20. To provide a means of settling disputes between partners (i.e. one wishes to terminate activity in public practice and other does not, disagreement over participation).			
21. As a means to terminate unprofitable clients.			
22. To become associated with friends of long standing.			
Other: _____			

CONCERNS OF MERGER CANDIDATE: A CHECKLIST[3]

	Great Significance	Some Significance	No Significance
1. The method of future income participation.			
2. Substantial differences in the factors used by the mergor in partner participation and or weights given various factors from those of the mergee.			

[3] *Id.*

	Great Significance	Some Significance	No Significance
3. Status of mergee's present partners, who may be too inexperienced to be assured partner status with mergor within a reasonable period of time.			
4. Compulsory retirement age for partners.			
5. Inadequate retirement program of mergor for mergee partners.			
6. Less income for mergee partners in years immediately following merger and/or inadequate recognition of the value of present practice.			
7. Smaller measure of managerial freedom and personal independence.			
8. Possibility of transfer to a distant city.			
9. Possible loss of name and identity in local community.			
10. "Agreement not to compete" clause in merger and/or partnership agreement.			
11. Inability to retain loyal staff members who do not meet mergor's standards.			
12. Differences in compensation of employees.			
13. The effects of the mergor's change in reports or other professional work on prior professional liability of mergee.			
14. Fees that may be required as a result of surviving organization's procedures and/or rates.			
15. Less direct partner contact with clients or need to shuffle clients to establish specialization.			

	Great Significance	Some Significance	No Significance
16. Future status of employees who have been offered partnerships by mergee in near future.			
17. Being "submerged" rather than "merged."			
18. Lack of cash flow immediately following merger.			

MERGER CRITERIA[4]
(Moss, Adams and Company, Seattle, Washington)

1. The merger will be mutually beneficial—that is, the advantages will outweigh the disadvantages for both the mergee and the mergor.
2. The parties to the merger will have compatible goals.
3. The people involved in the merger will be compatible.
4. A positive commitment will be made by all parties, based on full knowledge of all of the facts, to overcome the problems that may occur.
5. The merger is more advantageous than the alternatives of expanding an existing office or opening a new office.
6. The merger is consistent with our firm's long-range goals.

Other Considerations

During merger discussions there are obviously negotiation strategies and you want to make sure that you are sitting at the table as "equals." This is difficult when a firm is being acquired by a larger firm. However, it is very important during the meeting for both sides to feel very important and not like second-class citizens. If someone promises that you are going to receive a "piece of the rock," you should be very wary about such statements. If your firm is being courted by another firm, then, perhaps, you should plant the seed with other firms in the community to assure that you receive your worth.

As Lee Iacocca stated in his recent book,[5] always have a choice before making an important business decision. In other words, accept the best offer. Your firm should know firms that are interested in merging.

---

[4] *Id.*

[5] L. Iaccoca, Iacocca: An Autobiography (1984).

Because a firm scores low on the "Report Card" (which will be reproduced later on in the handbook), it may only receive one offer for the practice. However, if your firm has a specialty service and is one of the largest medium-sized firms in the city, then, obviously, you should receive more than one offer if you are in the merger arena.

During negotiations you should also seek outside counsel if you have never been through a merger or acquisition.

Finally, you should prepare a pro forma income statement to show the projected results of operations utilizing the hourly rate of the acquiring firm. The purpose of this exercise is to provide you with information that will improve your bargaining position for units and draw.

Questions and Answers

Question: When reviewing management charge hours, is there any area that should be reviewed more thoroughly than others?

Answer: Many CPA firms look at the number of charge hours; I believe that it is very important to review non-charge hours for the following reasons: (1) If the firm is managed by committee, then there may be a substantial number of hours devoted to meetings. Obviously, after the merger, these hours can be devoted to client development and obtaining charge hours; (2) If management does not properly use support staff or dictation equipment, a great deal of time is wasted in "pushing the pencil." Remember that it requires approximately eight hours to write what it would take one and one-half hours to say. (3) Partners sometimes are reluctant to charge all hours devoted to an engagement or do not keep adequate time records. Each firm interested in acquiring a practice should review non-charge time for potential hidden profits.

Question: Where can I obtain a list of firms that want to merge?

Answer: There are brokers who advertise in accounting publications. The *Journal of Accountancy* contains advertisements of merger candidates. Today, many individuals with their own relatively new practices are frustrated by high professional liability insurance premiums, staff turnover, and the highly competitive environment. Obtain the AICPA directory of firms for the past three years. When you review the directory, you will be able to identify the new firms that have started and then you can contact those firms to see if there is an interest in merging.

The local office of your state society would be another means to obtain names of firms that may be interested in merging.

Question: We have never had a signed partnership agreement. Some of our partners are hesitant to sign a partnership agreement because of the covenant not to compete. Is there any clause that can be used to finalize the agreement?

Answer: Sometimes partners don't execute a partnership agreement because of the covenant not to compete provision. The following is an example of a grandfather clause that can be incorporated in a partnership agreement. It is extremely important that a partnership agreement be executed before a firm starts to acquire other firms.

> *Example of grandfather clause:*
> The withdrawn Partner shall be entitled, *without payment to the firm,* to render services to clients whose aggregate average billings by the Partnership for the previous three years were not more than an amount (the "permitted amount") equal to the amount (the "Partner amount") set forth beside each Partner's name on exhibit _____.
> *If CPI index is included, this paragraph could be included:* "plus an amount equal to the Partner amount, multiplied by the percentage by which the Consumer Price Index as of December 31 of the measuring year shall have increased over the index as of December 31, _____."

Question: We are a firm interested in merging with a larger firm. There are two Big Eight firms in our area. Should we consider approaching all the Big Eight firms to determine their interest in acquiring our firm?

Answer: If your firm is very profitable, and has developed excellent professionals, I would recommend contacting all Big Eight firms. The firms that do not have a practice in the area may be interested in purchasing your practice to enter the market. Many firms have strategic plans, and, therefore, it would not hurt to contact either the executive office or the local office to determine whether the firm is interested in merging. On the other hand, the two local big eight offices should be interested in enhancing their own position in the marketplace. In certain situations a firm that does not have an office or is not a dominant firm in an area will pay more for a practice.

Question: Should the financial package include bar graphs and graphics?

Answer: When a firm is preparing information on a merger candidate, I recommend utilization of Lotus or some other software to prepare projections and other financial information. On the following pages, I have included examples of graphics that can be prepared utilizing Lotus.

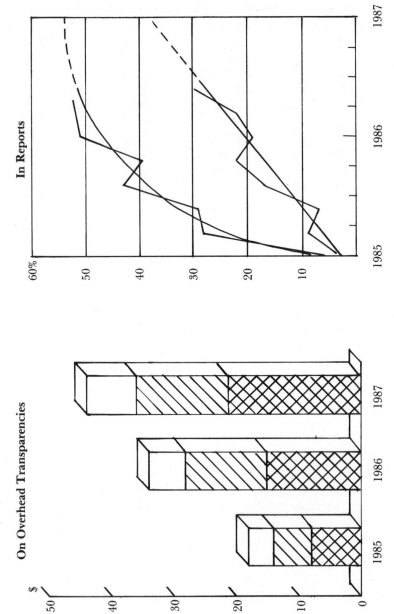

Successful Presentations Use Graphics

On Overhead Transparencies

In Reports

COST CENTER	PROJECTED BUDGET	ACTUAL BUDGET	DIFFERENCE
001	31,978	52,931	(20,953)
002	93,995	94,925	(930)
003	37,372	34,101	3,271
004	50,902	41,151	9,751
005	107,547	112,496	(4,949)
006	26,888	22,373	4,515
007	42,113	33,725	8,388
008	7,857	10,000	(2,143)
009	45,893	35,333	10,560
010	75,911	61,888	14,023
TOTAL	520,456	498,923	21,533

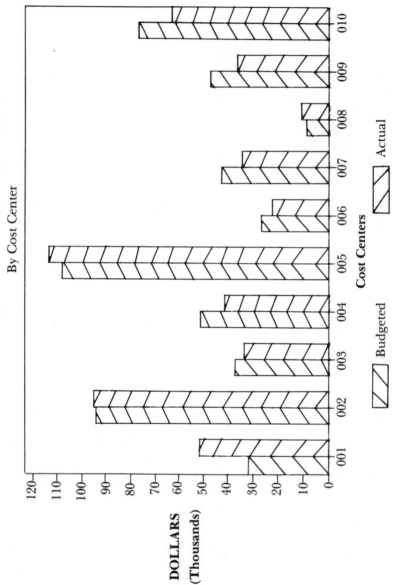

BUDGETED vs. ACTUAL — FISCAL YEAR 1985

By Cost Center

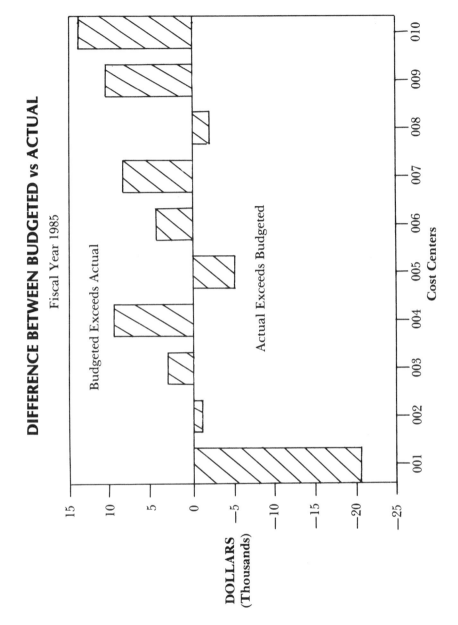

DIFFERENCE BETWEEN BUDGETED vs ACTUAL

Fiscal Year 1985

Budgeted Exceeds Actual

Actual Exceeds Budgeted

Cost Centers

DOLLARS
(Thousands)

Question: Our firm is interested in merging, but we are very concerned that the information will be leaked to our clients and staff. Is there any protection from this situation?

Answer: Obviously, it is difficult to keep such discussions quiet in a CPA firm because of the grapevine. However, before any discussions are held, I would recommend that a memorandum of understanding be signed by the parties attending the initial meetings. The memorandum would state that the discussions are confidential and that financial data can only be reviewed by the parties privy to the initial discussion. As talks progress, the memorandum of understanding can change.

Question: What is the difference between a purchase or buyout and a merger?

Answer: A purchase of a firm occurs when a partner or proprietor wants to sell his practice and retire, or leave public accounting. A merger is a true combination of two or more firms, with all partners surviving as partners in the new firm. However, in a true sense, when a firm merges with another firm, it is an acquisition of the firm. A merger of comparable-size firms, such as the proposed merger between Price Waterhouse & Co. and Deloitte Haskins & Sells, was a complicated situation which involved a very thorough review of details. "I was a partner with Deloitte Haskins & Sells at the time of the proposed merger; I always wanted to know which federal identification number would be used." Since a true merger among equals is rare, I frequently use the word *acquire* instead of *merge.*

Selected Reading List

Avoiding Trauma: The CPA Firm Buy-Sell Agreement, CPA Digest 1 (Aug 1985).

Cracium, *Continuity of a Small Practice,* vol 4 no 10 Practicing CPA 1 (Oct 1982).

Mingle, *Making the Marriage Last,* vol 8 no 8 Practicing CPA 1 (Aug 1984).

Valuing an Accounting Practice

4

Questions and Answers
Selected Reading List
Appendix 4-1   Merger and Acquisition Report Card

How to value an accounting practice is a question frequently asked by CPA firms. How do you determine a firm's value? Should good will be part of the consideration? Should there be a cash payment at the time of a merger? Although percentage of gross receipts has been one of the methods frequently used to value a practice, it is not by any means the only one. Several professionals have suggested various factors which must be considered in the valuing process, but there is no standard formula to follow. At the end of this chapter is a list of various articles which have been published on valuing an accounting practice. Certain courts have also ruled on criteria used in valuing a CPA's interest in a firm when there are marital disputes. There are, however, different factors to be considered in each case. Keeping these variables in mind, the purpose of this section is to highlight some of the factors and issues pertinent to valuing an accounting practice.

Those sellers who place advertisements in the *Journal of Accountancy* usually ask a percentage of gross revenue for their practices. In assessing such an offer, it is very important to review the quality of earnings, including the number of hours required to generate the revenue. If a practice does not keep accurate records and you cannot determine the quality of the earnings, then either the practice should not be acquired or the price of the practice should be decreased substantially. An alternative would be to tie the purchase price to subsequent collections. However, the seller **must pay the price** for being a poor business person, not only in maintaining inadequate reports—but perhaps also in not making the required investment in office facilities and equipment needed to compete in today's environment.

In 1973, before I decided to start my own practice, I placed an ad in the *Journal of Accountancy*. The ad read, "PITTSBURGH CPA WANTS TO PURCHASE ACCOUNTING PRACTICE." There were three responses to the ad and I met with each sole practitioner. Each one wanted 100 per cent to 125 per cent of the gross volume payable over a five-year period. They also wanted to be phased out of the practice after one year. Since I was 32 and the sellers were on the average 65 (and had serviced their clients for years), I asked myself what would happen if I started to lose clients because they did not care for my style or new ideas. None of the practitioners would accept a reduction in price for the loss of clients, so, instead of purchasing a practice, I chose to start one without any clients or long-term financial obligations. What was the value of the practice of the three sole practitioners in this case? For me, it was not a good business decision so I did not pay the price. Maybe someone else did purchase the practice and paid the amount requested.

The December 1985 issue of the *Practical Accountant* contains an excellent article written by Nicholas J. Mastracchio, Jr., on how to value a professional practice.[1] This article examines the facts facing a young accountant who is considering purchasing an accounting practice. It offers some guidelines and numerous examples for reaching a fair valuation. It also includes the financial calculations that should be prepared before making such an important decision. However, the choice basically comes down to what a willing buyer will pay a seller for an accounting practice. There will always be situations where someone will pay more or less than he or she should have paid for a practice.

In addressing the valuation subject, it is important to look at what is taking place in many of the larger firms. Ten years ago, it was uncommon for partners in a large firm to leave the firm and start their own business. Today, many partners are leaving the large national firms to start their own practice or join another firm. When this occurs, there is generally a provision in the firm's partnership agreement for valuing a practice covering clientele withdrawn from the original firm. I have seen agreements that require such individuals to pay between 50 per cent and 150 per cent of the gross business taken. In some of the national firms' partnership agreements the percentage is not disclosed; it is determined through negotiation among the partners.

---

[1] Mastracchio Jr, *How to Value a Professional Practice*, vol 19 no 12 Prac Acct 22 (Dec 1985).

Obviously, there is an industry trend to utilize gross volume to value an accounting practice. However, some articles by noted experts in this area warn acquiring firms to stay away from multiples of gross revenue. This is basically the message of articles that have appeared in the *Journal of Accountancy* and state society publications. These experts feel that the key ingredient should be the profitability picture before distributions to partners. In other words, what is the quality of earnings?

The reason behind this philosophy is sound. Ten firms can gross $1 million, but the nature of the revenue and the hours required to generate the revenue can be different. The percentage of profit before partner distribution can fluctuate. Thus, a firm that nets 50 per cent of gross revenue would generally command a higher price than a firm that nets 25 per cent. If one expert says not to use gross revenue and another expert says to use gross revenue, is there a compromise?

In a special report published by *CPA Digest* in August 1985,[2] one noted expert, Sheldon Ames, stated that applying different multiples to each type of revenue is a better way than applying one multiplier to the firm's gross volume. The expert suggests,

> Break last year's gross revenue into component parts—tax, audit, MAS, etc.—and multiply each by factors that account for quality and future value of the service line:
>
> | | |
> |---|---|
> | Compilation Segment | × .75 |
> | Review | × .85 |
> | Audit | × 1.00 |
> | Tax Compliance | × .60 |
> | Tax Planning | × 1.25 |
> | Continuing MAS | × 1.50 |
>
> Then add 10%-15% as a kicker for going concern value, plus the FMV of tangible assets . . .[3]

This seems like a good compromise but what should the percentage be? If you ask other consultants to the CPA profession, they may give you different percentages. However, I certainly feel this method is better than using one multiplier. Such an exercise would enable the purchaser to pay for the quality of the earnings for each segment of revenue.

Unfortunately, many medium-sized CPA firms do not measure profit by department and, therefore, it requires additional time to gather this information. In arriving at a multiplier, a higher one (over 100 per cent,

---

[2] Huss, *What's it all Worth?*, CPA Digest Special Report (Aug 1985).

[3] *Id* 2.

for example) should obviously be given to the more profitable areas and a lower one (50 per cent, for example) should be given to write-up work. After going through this exercise the value of a firm can be determined. However, other factors should be considered in determining a firm's potential value.

1. *Quality of partner earnings:* If the net realizable hourly rate is in excess of $50 and the average partner earnings exceed $125,000 (this figure will change depending on the location), then a firm should grade well in this category. It is also important that the firm has made the investment in people and equipment.

2. *Quality of personnel:* Has the firm developed outstanding professionals—both in the partner group and the professional staff? Will the partners fit in from the standpoint of chemistry and professionalism? Does the firm have experienced personnel in all positions? It is a positive sign when a firm has outstanding partners and has also developed excellent professionals.

3. *Location—strategic:* If the CPA firm is strategically located in a growing area or is in an area where an acquiring firm does not have significant presence, then a high grade will be given to the firm for this category.

4. *Nature of clientele (specialties):* The clientele of a firm may include specialties such as serving health care and higher education institutions. The firm with a specialty should grade well in this category.

5. *Nature of services (MAS, Strategic Planning):* The nature of services rendered to clients, which services include strategic planning and management advisory services, is very important. If a firm has expertise in an area that can strengthen a department in the acquiring firm, it should also be graded high.

6. *Fee structure:* The hourly rate factors are important. The average net cash realizable rate of the acquired firm should be within 20 to 25 percentage points of the rate for the acquiring firm.

7. *Hours managed by partner:* If it is normal for each partner in a firm to supervise 10,000 hours and the potential acquisition partners are only supervising 4,000 hours, then, obviously, there is a problem which would result in a poor grade.

8. *Investment in office facilities and computer equipment:* It is a positive factor when an office has made a significant investment in equipment, computers, etc.

9. *Quality of services:* If the firm has had an excellent peer review, then it should grade well. Additionally, does the firm provide a whole range of services for clients and does it include excellent client service professionals?

10. *Firm stability:* The firm's stability is very important. For example,

have partners left the firm recently and taken a great deal of business? Has there been a great deal of turnover in the partnership ranks? Has there been stagnant growth over the last four years? These are all factors that should be taken into consideration in answering this question.

When a firm is interested in acquiring another firm, a merger report card can be prepared. Please refer to Appendix 4-1 for an example of the form and a case study that utilizes the form. Once the firm has been analyzed, the question of how much should be paid for the practice must be addressed. If a firm is well-managed and has a high rating in all of the aforementioned categories, then that firm may receive a premium for its practice, such as an advance cash payment to each partner to consummate the merger. This percentage is negotiated and would be in addition to the accrued capital account.

On the other hand, if there is a poor report card, then there may not be any goodwill. If a firm has spent a great deal of time and money in developing outstanding professionals, then this should also be a very important factor in determining the value of a practice. This is especially true of a firm that is less than five years old where the bottom line has not had time to reflect the return of the investment in people. In certain cases, the average partner earnings figure is the critical component. The higher the average, the more your firm is worth. If the average partner's income is low, then, normally, the practice is not worth much. A good business person will not pay for a business and pay a premium when it cannot be justified. Each of these areas must be thoroughly reviewed to have a basis for determining the quality of a practice.

If you want to learn more about the valuation of professional practices, I recommend that you read the *Equitable Distribution Reporter,* a publication of Aspen Publishers, Inc. 1600 Research Boulevard, Rockville, Maryland 20850. In October 1981 and June 1983, it published excellent articles about valuing professional practices.[4] In the June 1983 article there is discussion relating to use of incremental earnings as a means of valuing a professional service corporation. The following chart (which appeared in the 1983 article) illustrates the use of this concept.

---

[4] Hempstead, *Valuation of a Closely-Held Business,* vol 1 no 4 Equitable Distribution Rep 48 (Oct 1981); Schwechter & Quintero, *Valuation the Professional Service Corporation,* vol 3 no 12 Equitable Distribution Rep 142 (June 1983).

Valuation of John Doe, M.D., P.C.

	Amount	Component of Value
Net Assets		
Appraised value of assets	$215,750	
Liabilities	(27,500)	
		$188,250
Incremental Earnings		
Compensation realized		
by John Doe	415,000	
Industry norm	(112,000)	
	303,000	
Applicable income taxes	(151,500)	
Net income of John Doe,		
M.D., P.C.	12,733	
	164,233	
Capitalization Rate (1/15)	✕ 6.67	
		1,095,434
Value of John Doe, M.D., P.C.		$1,283,684[5]

This is another way that a practice can be valued. You can see that if your average partner income is below the industry norm, you will not realize much value for your goodwill.

Finally, there is the distribution of units in the new firm, but, again, this is negotiable. When reviewing this area the acquired partner should be informed regarding what units are assigned to a newly admitted partner and the applicable purchase price. Also, is good will included in the purchase price? Generally, the payment of good will may be waived for a merged partner.

In conclusion, if your firm is considering a merger and is being courted by a certain firm, let it be known to other firms that you are considering a merger. In his recent book,[6] Lee Iacocca states that having a choice before making an important decision is one of the principal rules in business. In short, a good businessperson always has more than one offer. Furthermore, to make sure that adequate value is received for

---

[5] Schwechter & Quintero, *supra* note 4, at 143 (reprinted with permission of Aspen Publishing Inc).

[6] L. Iaccoca, Iacocca: An Autobiography (1984).

a firm's practice, it is of paramount importance as a firm proceeds through the merger process to obtain outside opinions from persons knowledgeable in the process.

Questions and Answers

Question: If a firm with five outstanding senior accountants is going to merge with another firm, what is the value that could be assigned to those senior accountants?

Answer: If the acquiring firm needs senior accountants, it would have to pay a search firm 30 per cent of the salary of each senior accountant, so that they are basically eliminating this expense through merging with a firm of quality personnel.

Question: If a firm has made a significant investment in office equipment and computers, will it realize any return on this investment in a merger?

Answer: This will depend on whether your office will remain in existence after a merger. If it will, there should be an appraisal and you should receive credit for the appraisal value in your capital account. If your firm will move into the office of the acquiring firm, then you should send a letter to other CPA firms in your area regarding the sale of your furniture and library, which will not be moved to your new location. You should receive more value taking this approach.

Question: Are there certain documents of a firm that you can review to determine whether you are receiving proper value for your firm?

Answer: When you are at the negotiating table, ask the firm that wants to merge with you what its policy is regarding mergers, e.g., is there a standard agreement? What is the basis of the unit awards? If you look back at the demise of many of the second-tier firms that grew through the merger process, one of the main problems was that different people seemed to receive different deals depending on how tough they were in the negotiation process. Obviously, this led to many negative reactions from partners who sold their practices and then realized that others had a better deal. The engagement of an outside consultant knowledgeable in the area will help the firm to determine whether it is receiving proper value.

When proceeding with an acquisition or merger you must make sure that you receive just compensation for the actual worth of your firm. If you do not receive the fair market value and you proceed with a merger, then the chance of the merger working is slim. Do not merge if you do not receive value for what you have built over the years.

Question: I have spent many years building a CPA firm, and, by merging upstream with a regional or national firm, it seems that I am really not receiving any value for good will.

Answer: It is normal to exchange equity in your firm for equity in a large firm and not receive any cash consideration. Some national firms have a good will factor which is included in the value of each capital unit. The payment of the good will factor will generally be waived in a merger. However, if you are considering merging upstream and you will not be receiving any cash consideration for your practice, you should give serious consideration to why you are merging. In other words, why work for 20 years and receive nothing for the good will or for the value of the client list and the development of excellent personnel? Perhaps you could be included in the firm's retirement plan, which could be considered as a payment for good will.

Question: Will a large national or regional CPA firm pay cash (a percentage of gross fees) for a practice?

Answer: If the practice is located in a strategic area, is very profitable, and has excellent professionals, there may be a tendency for some of the larger firms to pay a percentage of gross fees. If you grade high on the merger questionnaire then your firm should receive some type of payment for good will. Today, there are well-managed, medium-sized CPA firms whose average earnings per partner are greater than for most Big Eight firms. It is customary for the partners in such a firm to receive cash in order for the merger to go through. Actually, this should serve as an incentive for current medium-sized firms to better manage their practices so they may be the beneficiaries of such cash arrangements. The merger syndrome is here and this serves as an incentive for firms to manage their practices in a more efficient and profitable manner.

Question: What happens when there may be a substantial difference between hourly rates of firms considering a merger?

Answer: If a firm with 100 professionals is acquiring a firm with 25 professionals, it is very important to review the hourly rate for both firms and know the net realizable (cash) hourly rates for both firms. In many cases, such an analysis will show a significant difference in the hourly rates charged by the two firms and it may require a two-to-three-year period for the acquired firm to increase its realizable rate from clients. It should be apparent from this exercise that a problem may exist and the merger may have to be called off if the variance is too significant. However, in your negotiations you can request that a provision be included in the merger agreement that the current hourly rate cannot be increased more than 10 per cent a year for the first three years. Obviously, this would help retain present clients who could decide to change CPA firms because of significant increases in their bills. This situation is of paramount importance when a firm merges with a large national firm.

Question: I am 29 years old, a partner in a small firm, and our firm is interested in acquiring a practice of a sole practitioner who is 60 years old and ready to retire. What are the issues that I should be concerned with before I spend a great deal of time on this matter?

Answer: You must immediately determine the nature of the clientele that you would be acquiring and whether the seller is interested in remaining with the firm for a period of at least two years while you become acclimated to the new clients. If his clientele is an older one, what would be their reaction if they were represented by a much younger person? Remember that people chemistry is very important.

If the sole practitioner was interested in selling out and leaving the area, then you may consider proceeding with the transaction with payments which would be based on subsequent collections during a period of years after the acquisition. In other words, the more the seller participates during the first year to retain certain clients, the more the seller would receive.

The worst scenario is if the seller dies unexpectedly after signing the agreement. This happened to me once, and I had to spend a great deal of time and effort trying to retain clients I had never had contact with.

You must also review the financial records to determine the profitability of the practice. Many sole practitioners do not keep adequate time records. Certain data is stored in their heads. In many cases, the hourly rates are low and could be raised during the first two years to make the practice more profitable. However, this increase must be one that will be accepted by the client. The next question would be whether family members are involved in the practice; if they are, there may be problems in the future. The clients know the family, and, if there are any remaining family members, they may leave the purchaser empty handed. For example, if a manager (family) leaves the firm after the merger is consummated, he could take several clients with him. If there is a manager or senior accountant (family) in the office, I would have any such persons execute a covenant not to compete stating that, if they left, they would pay for any business taken from the firm at the time you acquired the practice. These issues should be addressed with your attorney.

Finally, there should be many safety valves for the purchaser in an acquisition of this nature. On a positive note, this situation could present a fine opportunity for growth as long as the buy-sell agreement is solid.

Question: In analyzing a practice, for example, a three-partner $1 million practice, what are some of the areas that should be considered outside of the normal boilerplate ones?

Answer: It is extremely important to determine whether the three partners control the client base or whether they have semi-retired and shifted much of the work responsibility to the managers. If this is the case, the key personnel in the merger could be the managers. You want to make sure they are enthusiastic about it. You want to ensure the success of the merger by having the managers involved in the discussion. You want to avoid managers leaving, starting their own practices, and taking a tremendous amount of business away from the firm-making the merger a disaster.

Question: If I have a medium-sized firm that is interested in merging upstream, are there any financial projections that I should prepare other than the boilerplate ones?

Answer: If your firm is interested in merging upstream, it is extremely important for you to prepare a projection for the proposed merger. You should project your income for the year and then, in another column, reflect the current activity less the expenses that would be eliminated as a result of the merger, such as rent, legal expenses, professional liability insurance, and other expenses. There may have to be a rental charge for additional space depending upon the size of the merger; however, many times CPA firms have sufficient space to absorb several more employees. You should then prepare a projection at your standard hours at the new rates that will be charged, so that you have a better idea as to the profitability of the new operation.

The following is an example of a projection for a proposed merger for Keystone CPA firm. You will note there should be a significant contribution to the bottom line. It is important to know this so you can negotiate a better financial arrangement. You may also note in the projection that the reserve for write-downs was increased to almost 30 per cent. Despite that increase, there is still a significant contribution to the bottom line. Let's face it—most CPAs are good business people, and they are not going to proceed with a merger unless they can see the benefits at the bottom line.

KEYSTONE CPA FIRM
Projection For Proposed Merger

	Year Ended 12/31/86	Year Ended 12/31/87	Merged Firm At New Rates
1. GROSS FEES (24000 Hours)	1026000	1026000	1560000

2.	LESS RESERVE (15%)	153900	153900	486000
3.	NET FEES	872100	872100	1092000
4.	EXPENSES:			
5.	Salaries Prof.	277000	300000	300000
6.	Salaries Office	85500	50000	50000
7.	Rent	44500	-0-	-
8.	Payroll Taxes	22100	25000	25000
9.	Telephone	20000	20000	20000
10.	Client Expenses	19300	19300	19300
11.	Office Supplies	9800	9800	9800
12.	Legal Expenses	1600	-0-	-
13.	Ins-Employee Blue Cross	14000	14000	14000
14.	Ins-Employee Life & Dis.	4800	4800	4800
15.	Ins-Prof. Liability	1900	1900	1900
16.	Ins-Office	1900	1900	1900
17.	Partners T&E	15000	15000	15000
18.	Car Lease	9600	-0-	-
19.	Association Expenses	7000	-0-	-
20.	Interest Expense	6000	-0-	-
21.	Depreciation and Amortization	20300	-0-	-
22.	Equip, Repair, Main, Supplies	5500	-0-	-
23.	Dues, Sub & Pub	8600	-0-	-
24.	Books & Pub - Tax	4100	-0-	-
25.	Tax Processing Charges	19000	25000	25000
26.	Postage	3800	3800	3800
27.	Staff/Client Entertainment	1900	1400	1400
28.	Contributions	1900	-0-	-
29.	Outside Services	3800	3800	3800
30.	Taxes-Business Privilege	1900	1900	1900
31.	Meeting & Schooling	4300	4300	4300
32.	Employee Travel	1200	1200	1200
33.	Computer Expense	3000	3000	3000
34.	TOTAL EXPENSES	640800	506100	506100
35.	ESTIMATED PROFIT	241300	366000	585900

Question: If a firm has a significant client that represents approximately 20 per cent of the firm's revenue, are there any special financial arrangements that should be considered?

Answer: In that particular case, you may want to work out a special arrangement whereby a payout is based on continued service to that client. In other words, you receive a certain percentage of the fees for five years, for example.

Question: What is the best way to proceed with preparing the financial projection of the combined firms?

Answer: Use a PC and 1-2-3 for projections. Analyzing the numbers is an extremely important part of the overall merger consideration. A personal computer (PC) and excellent software like 1-2-3 by Lotus Development Corporation should be used to facilitate all financial analysis. When considering a merger, large amounts of information must be digested to get an accurate picture of the situation. PC software like 1-2-3 drastically reduces the time and effort necessary to produce analysis reports. Also, 1-2-3 has one major advantage: numeric information can be graphed for more striking and easier-to-read analysis.

I recommend creating the following reports with 1-2-3: outstanding accounts receivable and work-in-process, projected revenue, salary budgets, budgeted hours, and summary of partner salary versus profit (loss). After a report is created, you can graph the results and print out the graphs for an excellent analysis of the data.

The important point to remember is that preparation of projected financial statements must be prepared for the first years of the combined operation. Sometimes, in a merger of a fairly large firm with another large firm, there is the possibility that the acquired firm will collect its own receivables. Thus, the acquiring firm will need a tremendous amount of working capital to sustain operations for the next three to four months until such time that cash flow from the combined operations improves. Unfortunately, some partners do not like to take the time to prepare these projections, but if you want to make a marriage successful it is important to develop these projections. Analyzing them will certainly highlight subsequent problems.

Question: It seems that in a merger we often forget about the clients of the acquired firm. We feel that the merger is great for the firms, but we have not adequately explained to the clients the reason or purpose for the merger.

Answer: The successful mergers take this into consideration. The participants in unsuccessful mergers forget that clients have a right to choose who is going to represent them and, therefore, there must be an orchestrated plan to make sure the clients receive quality services after the merger. Clients should also be informed about why the combination has occurred. One recommendation is to engage an outside service to survey the clients that were previously serviced by the acquired firm regarding their reaction to the merger. This will not only assist the firm in the current merger, but also provide them with information for future mergers.

Question: If I have a practice to sell, how do I get the message out to the community? Should I advertise in the *Journal of Accountancy* and state society publications, or should I engage a professional broker?

Answer: In these situations, I think every firm knows and respects certain firms in an area, and has been able to work with the partners on professional association projects and other matters. It is highly advisable to merge with someone that you know rather than an unknown quantity. There is nothing wrong with hiring a professional broker to assist you in merging your practice or perhaps introduce you to firms that are interested in merging, but, for the most part, the seller should know the firm he or she may want to be associated with and can pursue this independently. If the particular firm is not interested, then an ad can be placed in the *Journal of Accountancy* or a state publication to give potential buyers information about the sale. Also, it should be noted that, because of today's entrepreneurial spirit, many CPAs want to start their own practices. It might sometimes be appropriate for an individual who wants to start a practice to purchase one, providing the price is reasonable and fair.

Question: If I want to sell my practice, and I have negotiated a payment of 150 per cent of the gross billing with 75 per cent at the closing and the remaining 75 percent to be paid over five years based on subsequent collections, is this a fair agreement?

Answer: This is a common agreement, especially if the seller is going to stay for a year to introduce the clients and make sure the transition is a smooth one and then leave the area. It is quite appropriate that the remaining 50 per cent of the purchase price be based on subsequent collections. Obviously, if this type of agreement is executed, the seller would be wise to consider a nominal consulting agreement for a three-year period which would keep the seller active to solidify the transfer of clients to the new firm. This is particularly true in the case of a sole practitioner.

Question: In analyzing a practice, are there any specific areas that should be reviewed to determine whether the firm may have various problems that have not surfaced?

Answer: If you request a list of the clients that have been lost during the last three years, with the client billings and the reason for losing the client, this will tell you whether the firm is servicing its clients. In today's marketing syndrome it is extremely important to service clients and for the CPA to be the doctor, basically caring for the client's fiscal health. Quite often in a growth-for-growth's-sake program, the firm is more interested in obtaining new business than in servicing existing business. This is not intentional, but it happens. If this is the scenario, and there are many clients that have left the firm during the last three years, then you must be careful about merging your practice with that firm because you may lose some of your valued clients. If the purchase price is based on subsequent collections, the seller is the loser in this situation.

Question: If a practitioner desires to sell a practice and has not main-tained adequate time records, and you are not able to determine the number of hours required to generate the revenue, should you proceed with the acquisition?

Answer: In most instances, I would recommend that unless the seller can determine the number of hours required to generate revenue, the practice should not be acquired. You may be purchasing a practice that requires a significant amount of time to generate little revenue and will take you away from more profitable and exciting engagements. If the seller still wants to sell at a bargain price, then, obviously, the buyer can make an intelligent business decision.

Question: If the seller purchases a practice and realizes that there is ap-proximately $50,000 of unprofitable business that includes preparing tax returns for nominal fees, would it be wise to sell this part of the practice?

Answer: Providing you have already reviewed the client list and decided that you don't want to service certain accounts, you might contact, for example, three different individuals who have recently started their own practices, and ask if they are interested in purchasing accounts of this nature to enable them to cross a volume threshold. I have seen certain cases where a firm would buy a practice and sell off some of it to pay the purchase price, and this was very effective. Clients would have left anyway in this particular case, so the buyer made a good busi-ness decision.

Question: As a sole practitioner, I am not interested in selling the prac-tice, but I am interested in entering into an agreement with another practitioner in case I become disabled or sick. Are there standard agreements of this nature?

Answer: There are practice continuation agreements, and, in Form III in Chapter 5, there is an example of such an agreement developed by a CPA firm.

Question: We have a practice that grosses over $1 million, but approxi-mately $75,000 of that amount is unprofitable. Should there be any plan before the merger regarding these particular clients?

Answer: Obviously, there will be a fallout of clients in a merger. What is important is that you want to control the fallout to the extent possi-ble. I always recommend that a firm prepare a summary of the clients with low profitability. I would recommend submitting a letter to sole practitioners or smaller firms in the area, as they may be interested in purchasing this part of the practice. In other words, you may receive only 50 per cent of the gross, but you are farther ahead.

Question: What do you think of the ads that appear in the *Journal of Accountancy* requesting 150 per cent to 200 per cent of gross revenue?

Answer: Each practice has to be investigated on its own merits to determine whether the practice is profitable and therefore commands a higher percentage of the gross. Recently, I met with a gentleman that bought a practice and paid 200 per cent of the gross revenue plus interest on the unpaid portion. After one year he decided that it was impossible to make money during the next five years. He asked for my opinion and, after reviewing the details, I basically said that I would minimize my losses and put the practice on the market. Unfortunately, some CPA will come along and pay an exorbitant amount for the practice. I was not trying to be cynical; he *did* engage me to assist him in this effort. CPAs must be very careful in this whole process, especially those who have never purchased a practice. Those with a dream of starting their own practice are sometimes better off joining an organization and allowing their practice to develop within that organization. They can be compensated for the business they develop for the firm.

Question: Can you provide us with a brief example of the projected income statement that should be prepared?

Answer: On the next page I have prepared a document comparing actual results for a CPA firm with projected budgets for the following two years. In your review of this schedule, you will note the information that appears at the bottom of the schedule which is pertinent data to interested parties. I recommend that such a schedule be prepared for each merger situation.

XYZ CPA FIRM - MERGER CANDIDATE
FINANCIAL INFORMATION
FOR THE YEARS ENDED DECEMBER 31, 1987, 1988 AND 1989

	Actual 12/31/87	% of Net	Projected Budget 12/31/88	% of Net	Projected Budget 12/31/89	% of Net
GROSS REVENUE						
Charge Hours	40,000		45,000		50,000	
Average Hourly Rate	$ 48.00		$ 52.00		$ 56.00	
Gross Fees	$1,920,000		$2,340,000		$2,800,000	
Reimbursable Expenses	55,000		75,000		100,000	
BILLABLE	1,975,000		2,415,000		2,900,000	
LESS:						
Write Downs (10%)	197,500		241,500		290,000	
NET FEES	1,777,500	100%	2,173,500	100%	2,610,000	100%
OPERATING EXPENSES:						
SALARIES:						
Partner Salaries (A)	355,500	20%	434,700	20%	522,000	20%
Professional Staff	479,925	27%	586,845	27%	704,700	27%
Other Salaries	124,425	7%	152,145	7%	182,700	7%
Other Personnel Costs	124,425	7%	152,145	7%	182,700	7%
Total - Salaries	1,084,275	64%	1,325,835	64%	1,592,100	61%
FACILITIES	106,650	6%	130,410	6%	156,600	6%
PRACTICE DEVELOPMENT	35,540	2%	43,470	2%	52,200	2%
PROF. LIABILITY INSURANCE	35,540	2%	43,470	2%	52,200	2%
DEPRECIATION	35,540	2%	43,470	2%	52,200	2%

INTEREST EXPENSE	17,770	1%	21,735	1%	26,100	1%
OTHER OPERATING EXPENSES	195,560	11%	239,085	11%	287,100	11%
TOTAL OPERATING EXPENSES	1,510,875	24%	1,847,475	24%	2,218,500	24%
NET INCOME* (B)	$ 266,625	15%	$ 326,025	15%	$ 391,500	15%
AVG REALIZABLE HOURLY RATE EXCLUDING EXPENSE REIMBURSEMENT	$ 43.06		$ 46.63		$ 54.20	
NUMBER OF PARTNERS (C)	4		4.5		5	
AVERAGE PARTNER INCOME (A+B÷C)	155,500		169,000		182,700	
FEE VOLUME PER PARTNER (ROUNDED)	$ 480,000		$ 520,000		$ 560,000	
HOURS MANAGED BY PARTNER	10,000		10,000		10,000	

*Before any tax provisions

Selected Reading List

Accounting Practice—Classification and Valuation, 5 Equitable Distribution Rep 61 (Dec 1984).

Business Interests, 3 Equitable Distribution Rep 112 (Dec 1982).

Hempstead, *Valuation of a Closely-Held Business,* 2 Equitable Distribution Rep 48 (Oct 1981).

Raggio, *Professional Goodwill and Professional Licenses as Property Subject to Distribution upon Dissolution of Marriage,* 16 Fam LQ _ (1982).

Schwechter & Quintero, *Valuing the Professional Service Corporation,* 3 Equitable Distribution Rep 142 (June 1983).

Valuing an Accounting Practice, 6 Practicing CPA 1 (Graham G. Goddard ed, 1982).

Appendix 4-1

<table>
<tr><td colspan="2">MERGER AND ACQUISITION
REPORT CARD</td></tr>
<tr><td>Considerations</td><td>YES OR NO</td></tr>
<tr><td>1. Quality of partner earnings</td><td></td></tr>
<tr><td>2. Quality of personnel</td><td></td></tr>
<tr><td>3. Location - strategic</td><td></td></tr>
<tr><td>4. Nature of clientele (specialties)</td><td></td></tr>
<tr><td>5. Nature of services (MAS, strategic planning)</td><td></td></tr>
<tr><td>6. Fee structure</td><td></td></tr>
<tr><td>7. Hours managed by partner</td><td></td></tr>
<tr><td>8. Investment in office facilities and computer equipment</td><td></td></tr>
<tr><td>9. Quality of services (peer review)</td><td></td></tr>
<tr><td>10. Firm stability</td><td></td></tr>
</table>

EXCELLENT PROSPECT   - 7 to 10
AVERAGE PROSPECT   - 4 to 6
POOR PROSPECT   - 0 to 3

Case Study

Facts: ABC is a CPA firm that has a volume of $3 million with seven partners. The percentage of profit before partner distribution is 40 per cent. It has had excellent growth and is a good quality firm. They are considering acquiring a $500,000 practice (XYZ firm) that has two partners and a net return of 20 per cent before partner distribution. XYZ firm has not developed professionals, has recently lost business, and is not in a strategic location. The managing partner of XYZ firm contacted ABC firm to determine whether there may be an interest.

The following report card was prepared for XYZ.

1. Quality of partner earnings—average earnings of $50,000   NO

2. Quality of personnel—no strong professionals, except for one partner   NO

3. Location—not strategic, firm is in the same city   NO

4. Nature of clientele—no specialities, normal services   NO

5. Nature of services—no MAS, strategic planning, or personal finance planning   NO

6. Fee structure—40% difference in hourly rate   NO

7. Hours managed by partner—$428,000 for ABC, $250,000 for XYZ   NO

8. Investment in office facilities and equipment—only one PC, no new equipment for the past five years   NO

9. Quality of service—partners are committed   YES

10. Firm's stability—no recent breakup   YES

The average partner earnings would be substantially lower than the earnings generated by the XYZ firm. XYZ firm has not developed outstanding personnel. There is no strategic location. The nature of the clientele does not include any specialty. There are no unusual services offered other than the traditional boilerplate services offered by CPA firms. The fee structure is not comparable with ABC and the average dollars managed are substantially different.

GRADE: 2-YES/8-NO POOR PROSPECT

Conclusion: In this case, the report card is not a good one so there is really no good will value. However, a pro forma should be prepared to determine what costs would be eliminated if XYZ moved into ABC's facilities. Additionally, it would be advisable to prepare a client list and fee schedule to determine client profitability. Perhaps the firm is losing money on audits because it is not using audit software. Despite the report card, one must investigate whether, through better management, it can enhance the bottom line. If such a possibility exists, the firm can decide whether to pursue the merger. However, generally, if a firm grades low it is not a wise business decision to acquire the practice.

Examples of Merger Agreements

5

Form I
Form II
Form III
Form IV

This chapter includes examples of agreements that can assist your firm in drafting your acquisition or merger agreement. There are four different agreements. After selecting the most appropriate one, it is very important to have legal counsel review all the salient provisions. Some firms will discuss merging with a firm for months and never execute a memorandum of understanding between the parties. To assist firms on both sides we have also included an example of such a memorandum of understanding.

Form I   Example of memorandum of understanding between firms

Form II   Example of memorandum of agreement between a sole practitioner and a medium-size firm

Form III   Agreement to merge upstream together with drafts of back liability insurance and covenant not to compete agreement

Form IV   Accountant's practice continuation agreement

Form I

MEMORANDUM OF UNDERSTANDING

This Memorandum of Understanding is entered into on this _____ day of _____, 19_____, between _____, partnership, providing certified public accountancy services and _____, a general partnership rendering certified public accountancy services:

WHEREAS, _____ has provided professional accountancy and related ancillary services for many years and now maintains its office in _____;

WHEREAS, the _____ Shareholders are _____, _____, _____, _____ and _____ and the _____ Directors are all of the _____ Shareholders and, in addition, _____;

WHEREAS, _____ has provided professional accountancy and related ancillary services for many years and now maintains its office in _____;

WHEREAS, the _____ Partners are _____, _____, _____, _____, _____ and _____;

WHEREAS, it is proposed for _____ and _____ to enter into a partnership which consolidates the practices of both firms and to conduct the business of the consolidated firms as one firm except as specifically stated to the contrary in this Memorandum;

WHEREAS, both parties understand that further analysis and inspection are necessary to enable both parties to satisfy themselves as to the standards of quality, financial obligations, and other matters pertaining to each separate firm and to agree on administrative and managerial matters not yet fully discussed;

WHEREAS, representatives of _____ and _____ have agreed, subject to the approval of the _____ and _____, on many administrative, management, structural and technical issues involved in a combination of their accountancy practices; and

WHEREAS, to accomplish both parties' wish to conclude this consolidation of their professional accountancy practices as soon as practicable, but no later than _____, 19_____, _____ and _____ have entered into this Memorandum of Understanding.

NOW, THEREFORE, in order to summarize this understanding and to proceed to effect the consolidation and in consideration of the mutual promises and covenants, the parties hereto agree as follows:

1.   APPROVAL. This Memorandum has been duly approved by its _____ and _____ in the case of _____ and its Partners in the case of _____.

2.   EFFECTIVE DATE. The effective date of the consolidation of the parties' professional accountancy practices shall be _____, 19_____.

3. STRUCTURE AND NAME. The structure of the consolidated practices shall be a general partnership ("New Partnership") with _____ and _____ (sometimes referred to as "firms") as the general partners to provide professional accountancy and ancillary services to the existing clients (date). New Partnership shall provide all professional services after _____, 19____, previously provided by _____ and _____. All employees of _____ (except its Director/employees) and _____ (except its Partners) shall become employees of New Partnership on _____, 19____. All management and administrative functions of the firms previously provided by _____ and _____ shall be provided by New Partnership beginning _____, 19____.

New Partnership shall be carried on under the name of _____. Reports issued by New Partnership shall be issued under the name of either:

_____ or _____.

4. PARTNERS, DIRECTORS AND SHAREHOLDERS. Each person who is a Partner, Shareholder and/or Director (an "owner") of _____ or _____ on the effective date shall remain so. Any subsequent changes in Partners of _____ or Directors or Shareholders of _____ shall be subject to the prior written approval of the other firm under its own rules and procedures.

5. OWNERSHIP OF NEW PARTNERSHIP. Partnership interests in New Partnership shall be owned by _____ and _____ in the same ratio as their respective capital contributions to New Partnership as provided in paragraph 8. There shall be provision for a retroactive adjustment based on actual collections of accounts receivable and work in process through _____, 19____.

6. VOTING. Notwithstanding the ratio of ownership of partnership interests in New Partnership between _____ and _____, each Director of _____ and each Partner of _____ shall have one vote in New Partnership. A majority vote of all these persons shall apply except where otherwise indicated herein. In the case of non-routine matters 2-4 and 8-10 identified in paragraph 9(b), a two-thirds (2/3) vote of all these persons shall apply; provided, however, that, if either _____ or _____ has previously approved the non-routine matter under its own rules and procedures by a two-thirds (2/3) vote of all its Directors or Partners, then the vote of a majority shall prevail.

7. FISCAL YEAR OF NEW PARTNERSHIP. New Partnership shall adopt the same fiscal years for tax and management purposes as used by _____.

8. CAPITALIZATION OF NEW PARTNERSHIP. New Partnership shall be capitalized by _____ and _____ as of _____, 19____) by their contributing the following assets to New Partnership and New Partnership's assumption of the following liabilities:

   (a) Client Accounts Receivable and Work in Process (Net of Allowance for Variances)
   (b) Interest Receivable from Clients
   (c) Client Accounts (that is, the right to service client accounts)
   (d) Operating Supplies
   (e) Liability for Payroll Taxes
   (f) Liability for Bank Lines of Credit for Operations
   (g) Liability for Unused Vacation and/or Sick Leave Of All Personnel

   All other assets and liabilities will not be contributed to or assumed by New Partnership, but will be retained by the existing firms (except that the assets represented by items (m), (n) and (p) shall be used by New Partnership and their upkeep or rental paid by New Partnership), and include:

   (h) Libraries in use as of _____, 19____
   (i) Furniture and Fixtures in Use as of _____, 19____
   (j) Liability for Retirement of Present or Former Partners of _____ and Shareholders/Directors of _____
   (k) Liability for Office Leases
   (l) Liability for Management Fees to Retired Shareholders/Directors of _____
   (m) Liability for Stock Redemption of _____ or Partnership Redemption of _____
   (n) All liabilities (whether alleged or not alleged as of the effective date) pertaining to professional services rendered by each firm before the effective date of this agreement.

   Further, both firms agree that their respective representatives shall meet before the effective date to add to or to delete from the foregoing list as new items are brought to their attention.

9. MANAGEMENT. The management of New Partnership shall be carried on as follows:

   (a) *Day to Day Business Activity.* The day to day, routine business of New Partnership shall be run by a Management Committee consisting of the Managing Partner/Director of each firm and the Managing Partner of New Partnership. Each firm shall elect its own Managing Partner/Director under its own rules and procedures by a vote of its partners/directors. New Partnership shall elect a Managing Partner by a vote as provided in paragraph 6. This committee shall be the "Management Committee" and may be expanded from time to time by a majority vote of New Partnership.

In addition, special committees shall be adopted with members appointed by the Management Committee for such routine purposes as the Management Committee may determine are necessary.

(b) *Non-Routine Matters.* The following matters shall be considered non-routine. Such matters shall be presented to the partners of New Partnership at a meeting reasonably called for said purpose for decision by a vote as provided in paragraph 6:

(1) Compensation Matters (both current and deferred) and Policies for the Partners of _____ and Shareholders/Directors of _____, other than allocation of the firms' respective shares of the profits of New Partnership.

(2) Admission of a new owner in _____ or _____.

(3) Termination of an existing owner of _____ or _____.

(4) Acquisition, merger or de-merger of a new office or firm.

(5) Any matter which would materially affect or expose any Partner of _____ or Shareholder or Director of _____ to personal liability under the professional liability rules in force from time to time in _____ or result in a substantive reduction in quality control of the work performed by New Partnership.

(6) The acquisition of equipment or change in operating procedures involving an expenditure of greater than one per cent of the prior year's volume of any firm or office of New Partnership.

(7) Location or relocation of firm offices (except for the pending relocation of _____'s offices).

(8) Any matters pertaining to reduction or substantive change in malpractice insurance or to litigation or threatened litigation against the firm.

(9) Change of name or legal structure of New Partnership or either firm.

(10) Matters pertaining to de-merger, dissolution or separation of New Partnership.

10. ESCAPE PLAN. If within three years after the effective date, unresolved disagreements arise between _____ and _____, provisions shall be made for a separation or dissolution of New Partnership. These provisions will have the effect as nearly as possible of re-establishing the status quo as it existed prior to the effective date of this agreement. The following shall be specifically provided for:

(a) Client Accounts - Clients which were serviced by one firm at the effective date of this agreement but which are retained by the other firm or clients having as a "business source" owners or personnel of one office serviced by the other office shall be purchased at a price equal to one times the annual net billing with said amount payable twenty percent down and the balance over five years at twelve percent per annum interest.

(b) Staff Recruited - Any staff which presently is located in one office but is retained by the other office or staff of one office which is later recruited by the other office subsequent to a separation shall require a payment by the other office at the time of separation measured by thirty-five percent of that individual's then annual salary including prior years bonus.

(c) Records - Client Records shall follow the office which services the client. Firm financial or client records subsequent to the date of separation shall be available to each firm having need of access to said records. Operating manuals, forms, computer programs, and other proprietary and/or copyrighted items shall remain the property of the office originating said records or documents and thereafter shall not be used by the other office.

(d) Equipment purchased subsequent to the effective date of this agreement and remaining at the date of separation shall be purchased from New Partnership at its' book value by the firm using it at that location. Equipment existing as of the effective date of this agreement shall be returned to the original firm owning such equipment. Supplies shall remain in the possession of the office possessing such supplies at the date of separation. Accounts receivable and work in process shall be withdrawn from the New Partnership by the office rendering the service to the client. Any difference in ending capital account shall be equalized by a note receivable/payable due over one year.

(e) Covenants not to compete will remain effective with respect to each firm's partners or shareholders/directors (and their respective employees) but will not be effective between firms; i.e. the partner of _____ will remain obligated on his covenant (and his partnership agreement) with _____ but said obligation will not be effective with regard to _____. Not withstanding the foregoing, each owner of each firm (_____ and _____) will covenant to each other not to compete for each firm's existing clients or staff. Cost of such competition shall be assessed to the competing party under the above indicated formula.

11. CLAIMS ARISING FROM PERFORMANCE OF SERVICES. _____ and _____ shall each agree to defend and hold the other harmless and to assume payment for all claims, costs and expenses, including attorneys' fees, which may arise from the performance of services or acts or omissions by them respectively before the effective date. The cost of all "prior acts" insurance necessary to indemnify the owners of each firm shall be independently borne by each respective firm.

12. ONE FIRM CONCEPT. _____ and _____ agree that they shall conduct themselves in such a manner that the New Partnership and its' offices and their respective owners and employees shall practice as a part of one unit, not as a collection or individual practices. However, it is recognized that changes to uniform policies and methods cannot be made immediately. The objective is to as soon as possible develop a joint effort in the following: continuing professional education, client development, development of new services and products, staff recruiting, manuals and personnel guides, financial management procedures and controls, evaluation of personnel including owners of each firm, and guidelines for standards of quality in performing professional services.

13. WARRANTIES. Each firm and its owners shall represent and warrant on the effective date that:

(a) To their knowledge there are no pending or threatened claims relating to prior performance or lack of performance of professional services.

(b) The respective financial statements for _____ as of _____, 19____ and for _____ as of _____, 19 ____ as provided to each other have been prepared in conformity with acceptable accounting practices on a consistent basis.

(c) There have not been any material changes in the financial situation of either firm from the date of the foregoing financial statements which may have caused either party to reconsider consummating the consolidation contemplated by this Memorandum.

(d) There has been no loss of a client with annual fees in excess of $_____ for _____ and $_____ for _____ during the period from each respective firm's last fiscal year end and no material loss of business during that period.

(e) The partnership agreement of _____ and the directors/shareholders agreement of _____ are in substantially the same form as previously represented by each party to the other or as subsequently modified and disclosed to the other party.

(f) With the possible exception of _____, all _____ partners intend to continue as a partner subsequent to the effective date. All _____ shareholders/directors intend to continue subsequent to the effective date.

(g) _____ and _____ warranty to each other that neither firm shall negotiate with any other party for a merger, sale, or combination of their practices with any other party during the pendency of this Memorandum. _____ and _____ have spent a substantial amount of time to date in working out the matters pertaining to this consolidation and would be severely damaged if either party began negotiations with another firm before definitively terminating this Memorandum.

14. PROVISIONS UNDER WHICH THIS MEMORANDUM SHALL NOT BECOME EFFECTIVE. _____ and _____ understand that this Memorandum shall not become effective if prior to the effective date, an event related to personnel, professional liability, or other matters shall occur with either _____ or _____ which shall materially effect the practice of either firm. It is further understood that this Memorandum is subject to an approval by both _____ directors and _____ partners before it becomes effective.

15. Confidentiality of Information. _____ and _____ each agree that all information received from each respective firm during the period of these discussions shall remain absolutely

confidential and shall not be disclosed to any other party without first receiving permission from the firm whose information it is desired by the other firm to disclose. Such information shall include financial matters, forms and procedures, legal agreements, and compensation plans.

IN WITNESS THEREOF, this Memorandum has been executed on the above date by and on behalf of _____ and _____ and their owners by their respective authorized parties.

_____

_____

Form II

MEMORANDUM OF AGREEMENT

STATE OF _____

COUNTY OF _____

THIS AGREEMENT made this _____ day of _____, _____, between _____, CPA, of _____, _____, hereinafter called _____; and _____, a partnership of _____, _____, hereinafter called _____.

WHEREAS, _____ is a proprietorship, and _____ is practicing as a Certified Public Accountant in _____, _____ under the name of _____, and is desirous of merging _____ practice with _____; and

WHEREAS, references herein to _____ used in the singular shall be a reference not only to the proprietorship but to _____, individually, including the covenants herein contained; and

WHEREAS, _____ is a partnership of Certified Public Accountants with its principal office in _____, _____ and is desirous of acquiring practice

NOW, THEREFORE, it is agreed as follows:

I. MERGER OF PRACTICE. _____ agrees to transfer to _____, upon the terms hereinafter specifically mentioned:

A. All of _____ business services provided by its office in _____, _____.

B. The client list furnished by _____, attached hereto as "Exhibit A," together with the working papers, tax returns, correspondence, depreciation schedules, permanent files and all other data and records pertaining to the clients of _____, including all of those listed in the exhibit.

C. Copies of all the ledgers, journals, statements and other records of _____ clients maintained by the firm.

D. The furniture and fixtures owned by _____ in his accounting office at _____, _____, and listed on the schedule attached as Exhibit B.

E. _____ will maintain his office in the space presently leased by _____ at _____, _____, _____.

II. NAME. The name under which the partnership will practice, including the practice in _____, effective _____ will be _____.

III. PARTNERS. In addition to the partners presently parties to _____ partnership agreement, _____ individually will become a partner in _____ effective _____, upon the following basis:

A. On _____, _____ will become a partner in _____ and will receive as salary under Section _____ of _____ partnership agreement an amount of _____ annually.

B. At the time that _____ becomes a partner in _____ he will receive ownership units as provided in Section _____ of _____ partnership agreement in the amount of _____ ownership units. These will be additional units as provided in Section _____. For the purpose of this merger, the allocation schedule will be effective as of _____ as to income allocation as well as capital requirements.

C. _____ will share in the income allocated as provided in Section _____ and _____ of the partnership agreement.

D. _____ will draw a minimum amount of _____ per month from the partnership. The drawings will be charged against the income credited to _____.

IV. PARTNERSHIP AGREEMENT. _____ agrees to execute the current _____ partnership agreement and to be bound by all of the terms and conditions of said agreement, except as same may be amended by the terms of this agreement. His participation in the partnership shall be as follows:

A. _____ will receive credit to his capital account for the net book value of the assets transferred to _____ as of _____, including cash, accounts receivable, work-in-progress, and other assets used in the practice. _____ will be credited with the net book value for the furniture and office machines used in the accounting practice listed on Exhibit _____. Any capital excess of deficiency will be dealt with consistent with Section _____ of the partnership agreement.

V. OPERATION OF THE _____ OFFICE. The office in _____ will be operated as an office of _____ pursuant to the following:

A. _____ will be a "small business" partner in the _____ office.

B. _____ time will be charged to clients at _____ per hour.

VI. EFFECTIVE DATE. The effective date of the merger shall be _____.

VII. PROPRIETORSHIP OF _____. The proprietorship will not practice as a Certified Public Accounting firm nor will _____ practice as a Certified Public Accountant except as a partner of _____, after _____, and for as long as he is a partner of _____, or receiving retirement benefits from _____.

VIII. ACCOUNTS RECEIVABLE AND WORK IN PROCESS. The accounts receivable of _____ as of _____ will become the property and asset of _____. Work in process of _____ at _____ will become the property and asset of _____ as collected. Accounts receivable and work-in-process that are not collected will be charged back to _____ capital account.

IX. REPRESENTATIONS AND COVENANTS. _____ represents and covenants as follows:

A. _____ has good and marketable title to all of the property and assets covered in this agreement and there are no encumbrances except for balances owed as shown on the _____ books.

B. _____ will satisfy any and all debts and obligations occurred through _____.

C. _____ is not a party to or threatened with any litigation, proceedings, or controversy before any court or administrative agency which might result in any adverse change in the business or assets of _____, and is not in default with respect to any judgment, order, decree, rule or regulation of any court, agency, or Certified Public Accounting Board.

X. MISCELLANEOUS.

A. _____ will pay dues for _____ to be a member of the American Institute of Certified Public Accountants and _____ State Society of Certified Public Accountants.

B. _____ will pay dues for _____ to be an active member of one country club and one civic club in _____.

C. _____ will pay automobile expenses of _____ per mile for out-of-town travel for _____ and will pay _____ per month for local in-town travel.

XI. COMPLETE AGREEMENT. This Agreement constitutes the entire agreement between the parties and no amendment shall be made except by written instrument executed by the parties. This Agreement shall be binding upon the parties, their heirs, successors, assigns and personal representatives.

IN WITNESS WHEREOF, the parties have hereunto set their hands and seals the day and year first above written.

By: _____

By: _____

Form III

AGREEMENT

AGREEMENT dated ——————— among ———————————————

————————————————————————————————— .

1. The practice of ——————— will be acquired by ——————— as of ——————— (the "acquisition date").
2. As of the acquisition date:
   a. ———————————————

   and ———————————, (hereinafter collectively called the "New Partners") will become partners of ———————. They will receive initially the following fixed annual distributions and capital units:

Fixed Annual Distribution	Capital Units

   Total   The net asset value of the capital units allotted to the New Partners as set forth above will be charged to their ——————— capital accounts. Good will value will be considered fully paid for all such units. "Fixed annual distribution," "capital units," "net assets value" and "good will value" are defined in the ——————— Memorandum of Agreement.

   b. ——————— will be employed as a manager by ———————. His compensation will be initially at an annual rate of ———————, plus managers' supplemental compensation. Other terms of his employment with ——————— will be consistent with policies applicable to ——————— managers generally.

   c. Designated accounts receivable and unbilled work in process of ———————, in an amount equal to the net unrealized receivables value amount included in the net asset value amount due ——————— for capital units allotted, and certain tangible assets of ——————— to be designated by ——————— will be transferred to ———————. Accounts receivable and unbilled work in process transferred will be valued at recorded amounts and tangible assets at book value, with no value assigned to stationery and supplies. An amount equal to the proportionate share thereof of each of the New Partners, as computed by ———————, will be credited to his ——————— capital account. Any amounts credited to the accounts of the New Partners in respect of accounts receivable or unbilled work in process which are not collected by _____ will be charged back to them in the same proportions as they were credited.

d. If persons who are previously partners or employees of _____ become partners or employees of _____ as a result of the acquisition by _____, such persons will be eligible for _____ pension benefits based on the date of their joining _____ through merger without regard to previous service with _____ or other organizations with the exception of _____ who have prior experience with _____ and are given credit therefor.

3. a. Any amounts due to _____ for capital units which remain unpaid after application of the amounts credited to the accounts of the New Partners pursuant to subparagraph (c) of Paragraph 2 will be paid by the New Partners to _____ in cash as soon as practicable after the acquisition date. If any New Partners need assistance in financing, _____ will use its best efforts to assist them through its Debit Balance Financing plan with _____.

b. Any proceeds received by _____ in respect of accounts receivable or unbilled work in process of _____ which are not transferred to _____ pursuant to subparagraph (c) of Paragraph 2 will be received and held by _____ as agent for _____ and remitted to _____ as soon as practicable.

4. If any of the New Partners terminates his association with _____ at his own instigation before _____ and prior to that date performs any service within _____ ordinarily considered as coming within the practice of public accounting, as a partner, employee or shareholder of any entity or in an individual capacity, he will not be entitled to any amount in the respect of his units upon the surrender thereof. If any of the New Partners terminates his association with _____ at his own instigation before _____, no part of the amount to which he is entitled for units surrendered will in any event be paid until _____. If the payment of any part of the amount to which he is entitled is delayed in accordance with the preceding sentence, on _____ interest will be paid on such part from the date on which it would have become payable to _____ computed at the rate specified in Article 8(B) of the _____ Memorandum of Agreement.

5. _____ will obtain "back liability" coverage under a profes-

sional indemnity insurance policy relative to any services performed prior to the acquisition date in an amount equal to the acquisition date in an amount equal to that carried by _____ as of the acquisition date. _____ shall not assume or be liable for any obligations or liabilities of _____ or of any of the New Partners or of _____; and each of them jointly and severally agrees to indemnify _____ and hold it harmless against any and all loss, claim, damage or liability arising out of or based upon any act done or omitted or any services performed by _____ prior to the acquisition date.

6. Prior to the acquisition date, the New Partners will notify the Managing Partner of _____ in writing concerning the following:

   a. Any questionable situations involving possible conflicts of interest or independence matters relating to the practice of _____ or _____. (This facilitates the resolution of these kinds of matters in a timely fashion prior to the acquisition date.)

   b. Any existing personal liabilities of his own other than those incurred in routine circumstances (not including, for instance, automobile, appliance, or home mortgage loans), together with a description of assets sufficient to outweigh the listed liabilities. (If a prospective partner is in a personal deficit net worth position, the matter must be disclosed for consideration and discussion prior to the acquisition date.)

   c. Any significant matters relating to his health.

7. The New Partners and _____ will use their best efforts to integrate successfully the _____ clients and personnel into the practice of _____.

8. The terms of this agreement are separate from and in addition to the provisions of the _____ Memorandum of Agreement, and, to the extent that the terms of this agreement are at variance with the Memorandum of Agreement, these terms shall prevail.

9. In the event of the death or separation from the _____ partnership of any of the New Partners prior to the acquisition date, this agreement shall be terminable by _____ at its option, without liability on the part of any party to any other.

10. As provided in the _____ Memorandum of Agreement, acceptance of this document is subject to authorization by the Policy Committee and the written approval of a majority in interest in the partnership. Request for such authorization and ratification will be made as expeditiously as possible. No public an-

nouncement of this transaction shall be made prior to
_____ obtaining such approval.

11. This agreement shall be binding upon and inure to the benefit of the parties hereto and their respective heirs, executors, personal representatives, successors and assigns, provided that _____ shall not assign any of its rights hereunder without the prior written consent of _____ and none of the other parties shall assign any of his or its rights hereunder without the prior written consent of _____.

12. This agreement constitutes the entire understanding, contract and agreement among the parties hereto relating to the subject matter of this agreement, and supersedes all prior oral and written understandings, contracts, agreements and commitments, if any, relating thereto.

Witness the due execution hereof.

Form IV

ACCOUNTANT'S
PRACTICE CONTINUATION AGREEMENT

This agreement made and concluded this ＿＿＿＿ day of
＿＿＿＿, 198＿＿ between CPA Firm, a partnership of Certified Public
Accountants, ＿＿＿＿＿＿＿＿＿ (hereinafter designated
and referred to as "CPA") and of＿＿＿＿＿＿＿＿, (hereinafter designated and referred to as "PRACTITIONER");
WITNESSETH:

WHEREAS, CPA has offices in the City of ＿＿＿＿＿＿ ;

WHEREAS, PRACTITIONER is engaged in the practice of Public
Accounting with offices in ＿＿＿＿＿＿＿＿＿＿ ;

WHEREAS, PRACTITIONER desires to make provisions to protect
this practice, clientele, and himself in the event of his temporary or
permanent, total or partial disability or death;

Now therefore, in consideration of this Agreement, the respective
parties undertakings herein, and other valuable considerations, the receipt of which are hereby mutually acknowledged each from the other,
the parties hereto covenant and agree each with the other as follows:

1. In the event of the PRACTITIONER's temporary or permanent,
total or partial disability or death, CPA shall immediately undertake
to render PRACTITIONER's normal services for PRACTITIONER's
clients insofar as such may be ethically and legally permissible.

2. Definitions:

a. Temporary disability shall be deemed to occur when due to
PRACTITIONER's illness, injury, or unavoidable absence
PRACTITIONER is unable to render his normal services and
PRACTITIONER has a reasonable expectation of being able to
return to normal practice within ＿＿＿＿ (＿＿＿＿) years;

b. Permanent disability shall be deemed to have the same
meaning as temporary disability except that PRACTITIONER
shall not have a reasonable expectation of being able to return
to normal practice;

c. Partial disability shall be deemed to be either a temporary
or permanent disability which disability will permit PRACTI-
TIONER to render services to fewer than his full clientele
and/or restricted services to all or part of PRACTITIONER's
clientele;

d. Total disability shall be deemed to be PRACTITIONER's
inability to render any services on either a temporary or permanent basis to any of PRACTITIONER's clientele.

3. In the event of PRACTITIONER's total or partial temporary disability CPA shall render such services to the clients of PRACTITION-

ER as PRACTITIONER and/or said clients shall request, for which PRACTITIONER monthly shall reimburse CPA in an amount equal to seventy-five percent (75%) of the normal hourly rate at which CPA is charging CPA's clients.

4. In the event of PRACTITIONER's total permanent disability CPA shall render such services as are required by any or all of PRACTITIONER's clientele who agree to retain CPA. CPA shall pay to PRACTITIONER an amount equal to _____ percent (_____%) per year for _____ (_____) years of all fees collected from such former client or clients of PRACTITIONER.

5. In the event of PRACTITIONER's partial permanent disability CPA shall assume the rendering of services to such clients who wish to transfer all of their account from PRACTITIONER to CPA. For such completely transferred accounts CPA shall pay an amount equal to _____ percent (_____%) per year for _____ (_____) years of all fees collected from such totally transferred clients. With respect to clients who do not wish to transfer all of their account from PRACTITIONER to CPA, and PRACTITIONER desires the assistance of CPA in whole or in part in rendering services to such retained clients, CPA shall perform such services as requested by PRACTITIONER for which PRACTITIONER monthly shall reimburse CPA for such services in an amount equal to _____ percent (_____%) of the normal hourly rate which at that time CPA is charging CPA's clients.

6. In the event of PRACTITIONER's death CPA agrees to immediately render any and all services to PRACTITIONER's clients to the extent that such clients shall desire to retain CPA's services. CPA shall pay PRACTITIONER's executor, administrator, personal representative, legatees, heirs-at-law or assigns an amount equal to _____ percent (_____%) per year for _____ years of all fees collected from PRACTITIONER's clients who retain CPA. Within six months (6) after any such death CPA shall supply PRACTITIONER's personal representatives with an estimate of the amount to be paid under this paragraph.

7. PRACTITIONER will at no time, during the term of this agreement, or during the time payments are being made to PRACTITIONER by CPA under paragraphs 4, 5, 6, and 11, do anything that could be construed as competition.

PRACTITIONER further agrees that he will be readily available to assist CPA for the purpose of an orderly transition and takeover of any clients which PRACTITIONER turns over to CPA; will use his influence with his clients in effecting an orderly transition; will advise and consult with CPA as to the nature and status of client's work; will use his best efforts in promoting the interest of CPA in maintaining compatible relationship with all of PRACTITIONER's clients, and further that he, his wife, and members of his family will do nothing in derogation, by act, word, or deed, of CPA's interest in any clients which PRACTITIONER has turned over to CPA. PRACTITIONER further agrees that violation of any of the above covenants will terminate any payments, present and future, due under paragraphs 4, 5, 6, and 11.

8. PRACTITIONER will make available to CPA, within thirty (30) days after execution of this Agreement, a list of PRACTITIONER's clients and a description of the type of services normally performed for each client.

9. Within thirty (30) days after execution hereof PRACTITIONER shall inform his clients of the existence and nature of this AGREEMENT, and introduce a representative of CPA to his clients.

10. PRACTITIONER shall keep accurate records and work papers of the services PRACTITIONER performs and shall keep these records in such a manner as they will be readily available to CPA when and if needed. Such records shall include, but are not necessarily limited to, working papers, analysis sheets, depreciation schedules, adjusting entries, trial balances, financial statements, copies of tax returns, as well as records of accounts receivable of clients and work in process but not completed.

11. PRACTITIONER, in the event of any disability set out above, to the extend that PRACTITIONER's physical condition permits, will assist and cooperate with CPA in CPA's performing such services on behalf of PRACTITIONER.

12. In the event PRACTITIONER desires to discontinue rendering services to any given client while otherwise not under disability and actively engaged in practice, PRACTITIONER shall refer any and all such clients to CPA. In the event such clients retain CPA, CPA shall pay to PRACTITIONER the same amounts as set forth above in the event of PRACTITIONER's death.

13. In the event of PRACTITIONER's retirement or any of the disabilities set forth above. PRACTITIONER shall do all those things ethically, legally and reasonably necessary to persuade and/or influence PRACTITIONER's clients to retain CPA's services. PRACTITIONER shall not permit PRACTITIONER's staff, employees, immediate family, nor personal representatives to make derogatory statements concerning CPA or any partner or member of its staff nor to otherwise hinder the orderly, efficient, and expeditious transfer or assumption of the right to PRACTITIONER's practice.

14. In the event PRACTITIONER fails to perform any of PRACTITIONER's undertakings herein, any periodic payments due or to become due under this agreement shall be terminated.

15. It is expressly understood that nothing herein will be deemed to make PRACTITIONER other than an independent PRACTITIONER, and PRACTITIONER shall not be deemed to be a partner, member, employee, or agent of CPA.

16. CPA upon demand of PRACTITIONER's personal representative, in the event of PRACTITIONER's death, shall purchase PRACTITIONER's office furniture and equipment at a price to be agreed upon or, if no agreement is made, at a price to be determined by an independent, knowledgeable appraiser.

17. Any amounts due PRACTITIONER or PRACTITIONER's personal representative from CPA shall be payable:

    A. On an annual basis _____ (_____) days after the close of CPA's fiscal year;

    B. On a monthly basis _____ (_____) days after the last day of the month;

    C. On a purchase pursuant to paragraph "16" above, upon delivery of said chattels.

18. Any amounts due CPA from PRACTITIONER shall be payable on a monthly basis _____ (_____) days after the last day of the month.

19. This agreement shall be binding on CPA and PRACTITIONER's legatees, distributees, heirs, successors, and assigns.

20. This Agreement may be terminated by either party upon thirty (30) days written notice by either party, however, without prejudice to collectibility of amounts due for services under transactions completed prior to termination.

"PRACTITIONER"

CPA Firm

by _____

Managing Partner

Note: This agreement is a prototype of one developed by Rea & Associates, Inc.

Question: Should a noncompete agreement be executed by a professional in a CPA firm?

Answer: This is a situation that generates opposing views, on the subject and there is also a question of legality. For Example, are noncompete agreements legally enforceable? Generally, the response is, "Individual state law governs this particular issue." The Judicial system normally will not Enforce an unreasonable agreement that would restrict an individual from performing responsibilities in a given state, and, thus, preventing an individual from earning a living. A CPA practice is extremely valuable, and I believe that it is important to protect the value via such noncomplete agreements, which should be executed by senior people, managers, and partners. Again, the purpose is not to prevent the individual from practicing, but for the firm to receive some compensation for clients taken by the individuals leaving the firm. In the February, 1986 issue of the practicing CPA, there was an excellent article about this subject. The article contained two opposing views prepared by consultants J.N. Nisberg and Morris L. Shifman. I would strongly recommend that every practitioner read this article (*Compete or Non-Compete: That is the Question,* The Practicing CPA, February, 1986, at 6, 7).

Human Resource Management: Planning for Merger Shockwaves

6

Questions and Answers
Selected Reading List
Appendix 6-1 Productivity and Profitability

As mentioned at the beginning of this handbook, mergers and acquisitions are occurring at such a rate that few companies can safely assume immunity from some sort of business combination. No one within the accounting profession needs to be convinced of this. Every CPA firm in the country should prepare itself for a future merger by developing a solid merger and acquisition plan. This chapter focuses on the "human" factors involved in such a plan. Ordinarily, merger planning and decision making are based most heavily on the financial considerations involved. However, people play the key role in the success of any given combination of CPA firms. Recognizing the importance of human resources in engineering a merger should be part of every business plan.

Planning for the psychological "shockwaves" inherent in any type of merger may make the difference between short-term setbacks and the future success of a new firm. It is clear that a firm may increase its power by combining with another practice, but consideration should be given to more than the combination's "structural" compatibility. A merger represents a starting point insofar as it calls for some kind of reorganizing and restructuring of one or both firms. Mergers create new problems as well as new possibilities. While a merger may revive a financially ailing firm or enable entry into a new technology or marketplace, it also creates an organizational shake-up. Often a new combination results in a change in operating style. This change can be a positive event for many firms if it is planned for. Fresh ideas, new blood, and the additional energies a merger brings can be key ingredients in the future success of a new combination. Ideally, mergers and acquisitions should be used for morale building, attitude improvement, innovation, and increased productivity. But without deliberate, strategic planning directed toward these goals, a company is likely to be affected along negative lines as people begin to feel fearful, threatened, and anxious.

Since much of the merger activity between small and medium-sized CPA firms in the United States goes unreported, it is difficult to obtain a precise set of statistics regarding their success rate. Available statistics, however, generally indicate that growth through acquisition is a risky business. On the whole, acquirers have less than a 50 percent chance of being successful in their merger/acquisition ventures. Studies conducted on those companies describing their acquisition efforts as unsuccessful most frequently point to "management" as the main reason for a high percentage of merger difficulties and failures. Inadequate or inaccurate pre-acquisition research, absence of a well-developed integration plan, loss of key management talent, and lack of follow-up were cited as the major reasons for the "people problems" that necessarily occur with a new combination.

Professionals claim anywhere from one-third to one-half of all mergers fail to realize anticipated financial expectations, at least in part due to personnel problems. What are some of these problems and how should they be handled? We shall go on to present some of the human factors involved in the merging process and then discuss how they can be incorporated into a strategic business plan.

While each merger agreement is in some respects unique, there are a remarkable number of features they all have in common. Even when mergers and acquisitions involve two companies in the same industry, there can be dramatic cultural differences. Unless these differences are recognized, understood, and dealt with astutely in the integration efforts, the risk of failure increases significantly. Corporate culture is a peculiar blend of an organization's values, traditions, beliefs, and priorities. It is a sociological dimension that shapes management style as well as operating philosophies and practices. One of the most common merger problems is the "violation of expectations" that alienates people in the acquisition. As priorities blur and inconsistencies appear between new approaches and the old way of doing business, culture shock sets in. People first become confused, then frustrated, then resistant to change.

By their very nature, mergers and acquisitions foster times of uncertainty and insecurity. Invariably, the employee reaction to this ambiguity destabilizes organizations and creates dissonance. Dissonance occurs when there is a significant discrepancy between (1) what is perceived as the actual state and (2) the desired condition of an organization. Top executives must move decisively and purposefully—not simply to make changes, but to make the right changes and then to intelligently manage the organizational dissonance that is created. The best steps obviously are the preventative ones. Dissonance is not something to be stifled, sidestepped, or ignored. A strategic game plan is essential. A categorization of different merger/acquisition situations makes it much easier for management to anticipate the problems that are most likely to occur. The type of acquisition determines to a large extent how severe the blow is, how long the trauma lasts, and the extent of damage that is done to a firm's health. In his book, *After the Merger: Managing the Shockwaves* (1985), Price Pritchett identifies four types of acquisitional postures: (1) rescue, (2) collaboration, (3) contested situation, and (4) raid. Each combination has its own idiosyncrasies and unique implications regarding how management should gear up to cope with the difficulties that routinely develop.

Employee performance during the postmerger period can be predicted with alarming certainty. The graph included as Appendix 6-1 charts the common pattern of organizational performance during the first two years following acquisition. Operating effectiveness is sabotaged by the psychological shockwaves and reactions of employees. Employees at *all* levels are concerned with the future. From the partners down to the staff, employees are wondering how the combination will affect their jobs. Will I be promoted, demoted, or even terminated? Will I have to relocate? Will my benefits be reduced? Often, however, these fears are silent. When employees feel threatened, their trust level is low and their behavior is self-defensive. Communication deteriorates and the truth is easily distorted by rumors and gossip. Emotions dominate and people act irrationally. Self-preservation overrides the firm's goals and productivity decreases sharply. Once employees are allowed to develop a "me against them" attitude, the future of the firm is threatened.

David Robino and Kenneth DeMuse, specialists in human relations, recently conducted a study on human resource management during a merger or acquisition (see Suggested Reading List at the end of this chapter). They conducted a global survey of the personnel managers of a diverse group of both *acquiring* and *acquired* companies. The overall results of the study indicated that it was only *after* a merger or acquisition that the respective groups discovered the significance that human resources had for its eventual success or failure. Managers attested to the discontentment of employees and stressed the need for human resource professionals to help other members of management recognize the importance of the human element in the eventual success of a merger.

There was general agreement that the personnel function must move beyond the administrative activities of employment, labor relations, compensation and benefits, and so on and expand into the broader areas of overall human resource management. Respondents stressed the need for honest, open, and responsive communication in order to squelch rumors and relieve anxiety among employees. Early involvement, sound management principles, and honest communication were among those recommendations most frequently made by management of both acquiring and acquired organizations.

In any attempt to apply these observations to the CPA profession, one must keep in mind that many small and medium-sized firms do not even have a personnel department. In most cases it is the partner of a CPA firm who must become aware of the human factor and implement a strategy accordingly, that is to say, it is the partner's responsibility to consider human relations or "people chemistry" in the actual development of a merger and acquisition plan. Prior to the decision to merge, even before negotiations, a partner must recognize that people are a firm's most valuable resource and that people chemistry is of paramount importance. Understanding people is the first step in utilizing them effectively. Following are some communication tips which should be taken into account in the merging and acquisition strategy of any firm.

Basically, firms should be aware of the "human factor" at three stages of the merging process:

1.   In the actual decision making when a merger is being considered

2.   During the negotiation process

3.   In adopting postmerger management policies

Before making a decision to merge it is mandatory that you come to know the "personality" of the other firm. The voice of experience warns you again to beware of those firms offering you a sure thing. There are certain things you should know even before you negotiate. In those cases where an outside consultant is employed to assist a firm in its decision whether to merge, part of the engagement should include an analysis of people chemistry.

The success of any organization depends on building the right team; this requires a combination of talent and training. In order to achieve organizational goals and avoid personnel problems, a firm must learn to utilize the strengths of each individual. One tool which enables an employer to identify these strengths is the Predictive Index System (PI) Developed by Arnold Daniels, PI is an assessment tool that helps management to identify the best qualified people for specific jobs. Not only does PI help companies hire the right people but it enables employers to train individuals according to their proper potential. PI could be used to obtain psychological profiles of potential partners in a merger and their support staff. If the results of this analysis indicate a lack of compatibility, then you may be preventing a future failure by deciding not to proceed any further. Robert L. Coker, former managing partner of Clifton, Gunderson & Co., recalls that his firm was so concerned about the types of people coming in as partners as the result of mergers that they used to use psychological testing on all incoming partners before they completed the merger agreement. While this approach was later abandoned, the claims "it might not have been a bad idea to have continued it."[1]

Dr. Rex Gatto developed another assessment instrument, "Interpersonal Working Associations Inventory" (IWAI) (see Suggested Reading List at the end of this chapter). IWAI is a guide to what Gatto calls "firm building." It is extremely applicable in a merger situation. He describes firm building as clearly establishing: firm-wide expectations, open, honest, trusting, and respectful communication; responsibilities for each employee; a recognition system for employees; a method to encourage employees to speak out; a safe environment in which to work; a method to solve problems; a collective understanding of what the merger involves for each employee (partners, managers, senior accountants, semi-senior accountants) to succeed; and trust.

The IWAI lets all members of a firm give feedback to themselves and their coworkers. The instrument gives feedback on communication, time management, technical skills, and team building. Gatto's concept of feedback is to feed the future, and to be pro-active in addressing issues. Use of this assessment instrument enhances communication and job productivity because information is clearly given to working associates (partners, managers, accountants, semi-seniors); there is less distortion of information. This moves the firm to a better understanding of the working personality by removing information blockage.

This leads to the most powerful aspect of firm building: establishing trust among all the partners, managers, and support staff.

When proceeding without the professional consultant, however, the

---

[1] The Practical Accountant, March 1981.

best way to acclimate yourself to another practice is to take a tour of its office. Be observant; there is a lot you can determine from the atmosphere of an office. For example, do you hear laughter? Do you sense a positive or negative atmosphere? I once took a tour through the office of a firm that was going to merge with another firm. I could see immediately that the office manager and secretary were not people-oriented. Given the support staff and type of people working for the firm that wanted to acquire this one, I could see immediately that there would be definite problems with the support staff. My suspicions were confirmed when I spoke to one of the partners about one of the individuals in question. A person may have to be counseled and possibly terminated for the sake of the merger. You should make several visits to the office. Make sure you examine the entire facility and meet everyone. Is there general enthusiasm for the merger? Is there a sense of insecurity? Observe how the employees react to you, how they are working, and whether they have a positive or negative attitude. Partners, managers, and perhaps even senior accountants should have the opportunity to meet the representatives from the other firm. It is important that they get to know each other during the discussions and negotiations. In today's business environment it is ludicrous *not* to introduce managers and staff until the business agreement is signed. Client retention and development and, consequently, the future of the combined firm will depend on the personality of the partner and manager group. Remember, the worst scenario is to merge and then have a few managers leave after the merger to start their own firm. If such managers control a significant client base, the firms may have merged but lost good people and clients.

If you want to know the personality of a firm, you must ask salient questions, even before negotiation proceedings. For example, you need to know if there has been a great deal of turnover within a firm. If there has, you must then determine if it is controlled or whether there is a revolving-door scenario. When it is controlled, periodic turnover may be healthy for a firm. In the case of a revolving door, however, turnover is uncontrolled and a sign of poor people management.

It is important to examine the policy manual of the other firm for the same reason. You may have to adjust salaries to cover any loss of fringe benefits.

After you have gathered the necessary information on a firm and decided to proceed with negotiations, do not lose sight of the human factor. People chemistry will be the most important sign during merger negotiations. It can be as bad to be offered the world as it is to be treated like a second-class citizen. If there is a conflict during bargaining, such as over the name of the new firm, for example, this is a sure sign of future problems.

Insist on documenting everything during negotiations. Adopt a plan and stick to it.

When a firm decides to merge partners from another firm, it should be very careful to review their backgrounds to make sure these individuals are solid citizens in all respects, particularly in relation to their financial health (e.g., have they personally guaranteed many loans?). In a merger, sometimes a partner in one firm becomes a manager in the combined firm. This is a demotion, and one that certainly has negative effects on both the individual and his or her family. In such a case, it probably would be better for the individual to withdraw from the firm and go solo or join forces with another firm. Such decisions must be planned carefully in order not to disrupt the operation. Management should use well-defined criteria in making staffing decisions. If the merger has brought about departmental overlap or duplicated functions, an early evaluation will indicate which person is better suited for the position. Also, the acquirer needs to know where promotion potential exists to assure good management succession planning. A merger virtually always leads to some early turnover in key management positions, and decisions must be made regarding promotions, transfers, and recruitment of new blood. High-talent people, in particular, will often opt for immediate guarantees they can negotiate with a new employer rather than wait out the merger situation and gamble that their careers will be well served by the acquisition of their firm. In those situations where certain employees will have to leave, it is equally important to provide for a smooth transition. While honesty is the best policy, many of the larger firms try to assist those who must go by helping them to find new jobs, offering attractive severance packages, and even arranging for counseling. The impact that termination can have on employees (particularly the managers) and their families should not be underestimated.

Finally, in adopting postmerger management principles, it is best to begin by informing employees of their future as honestly and as soon as possible. This prevents misunderstandings and gives them time to plan for any adjustments they may have to make. Respondents to the merger and acquisition survey cited honest communication as the single most important ingredient in the success of any combination. Informing employees of their role in the new combination will assist in the overall flow of the operation. Personal contact via meetings will help to prevent the discontentment that often leads to the "we/they" attitude and stands in the way of productivity. There should be a meeting of all the professional staff of both firms immediately following the merger announcement and enthusiasm must be evident during the meeting.

For a final word on making the "marriage" work, it is essential to stress the need to *motivate* employees. Employees at all levels have attitudes and opinions they personally consider important, and they must be given the opportunity to share their feelings, offer constructive ideas, or ventilate concerns. Employees in the acquired firm will be extremely sensitive to how they are being treated and will perform better if management: (1) presents well-defined expectations, and (2) communicates confidence in their ability to measure up. Management should be involved in team-building efforts in order to overcome the inter- or intracompany difficulties which interfere with the organization's overall functioning. In short, the team-building process is designed to:

> Help people learn how to work together
>
> Improve communications
>
> Clarify priorities and define objectives
>
> Overcome role ambiguity
>
> Identify problem areas and sources of conflict
>
> Build trust and group strength

Today, many organizations throughout the country offer team-building (or, as Dr. Gatto refers to them, "firm building") sessions for merged companies. These and other educational programs will help to solidify the merger by training and orienting staff toward more productive, efficient performance.

In summary, each firm must give undivided attention to determining whether the management philosophies and combined people chemistry of both firms are compatible. If they are not, then the firms probably should not merge.

Questions and Answers

Question: Is there such a thing as a people merger?

Answer: Yes, if a firm's bottom line is average but it has developed outstanding professionals, a merger can and often will be consummated. Remember, this is a service business and excellent professionals are at a premium. There is a value for well-trained professionals. For example, if you have three outstanding senior accountants who will probably be promoted to manager in the very near future, what would their value be? Today, CPA firms are paying search firms 25 per cent of the first year's salary for an experienced senior accountant. If each senior earns $30,000 per year, their combined salary would be $90,000. Twenty-five per cent of this figure would be $22,500, which would be the savings of the acquiring firm. If CPA firms develop solid professionals, the value of the practice will definitely be enhanced.

Question: What are the ingredients for a successful merger?

Answer: The successful merger must have good people, comparable economics, strong leadership at the top to guide the merger, and also clients that will mesh in with the new firm and allow the acquiring firm to provide additional services through its expanded staff and re- sources.

Selected Reading List

Coker, *Some Practical Tips on Buying or Merging an Accounting Practice,* 14 Prac Acct 205 (Mar 1981).

A. Daniels, The Predictive Index System (1955)

R.P. Gatto, Interpersonal Working Associations Inventory (1987).

Hamilton, *HRD Value in Mergers and Acquisitions,* Training & Dev J 31 (June 1986).

J.R. Noland, Personalysis (1983).

P. Pritchett, After the Merger: Managing the Shockwaves (1985).

Robino & DeMuse, *Corporate Mergers and Acquisitions: Their Impact on HRM,* 30-11 Personnel Admin 33-44 (Nov 1985).

Appendix 6-1*

Productivity and Profitability

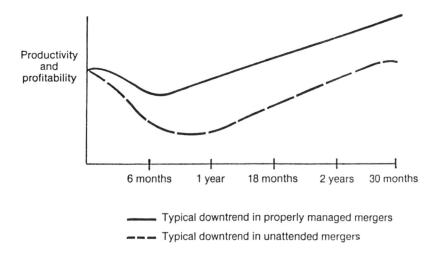

Productivity
and
profitability

6 months   1 year   18 months   2 years   30 months

——— Typical downtrend in properly managed mergers

– – – Typical downtrend in unattended mergers

---

* P. Pritchett, After the Merger: Managing the Shockwaves (1985) (reprinted with permission).

Dissolution of a Merger

7

Sample Form
Questions and Answers

Sometimes a merger is consummated without proper planning, and an eventual de-merger may occur. There are also firms that carefully plan the merger only to discover that the partners can't get along and, again, a de-merger occurs. This is a true story told to me by a managing partner. When our firm started to grow, we felt it necessary to strengthen our tax practice, so we decided to admit a tax partner who was with a Big Eight firm. We met several times prior to merging and eventually came to an agreement.

However, after three months I knew we had made a poor decision. We had just been asked to submit a proposal to a potential client, and a team from our office visited the prospective client. We were notified shortly thereafter that we obtained the engagement and immediately this new partner came into my office and said, "That engagement should be on my billing run as I really helped get the engagement." I knew right away that he was not a team player. I should have made a decision then to terminate the merger, but it existed for another couple of years until I came back from my mother's funeral. Her death was totally unexpected. The first words spoken were "Well, now that you're back you can get your billing out." There was absolutely no compassion whatsoever. Shortly thereafter that partner decided to leave with another gentleman from our firm to start a new firm. We had a de-merger agreement within one week and life moved on for all of us. Subsequently that firm de-merged and litigation has been proceeding for the last few years. I firmly believe that life is too short to work with individuals that do not share the same philosophy or cannot communicate with each other.

Previous chapters have discussed the problems associated with the dissolution of a firm, particularly with a longstanding firm such as Lester Witte & Company, Clarence Rainess, and others noted in Chapter 1. The important point to remember is that firms must spend a significant amount of time getting to know each other before the marriage is consummated. I will never understand why a person dates a prospective spouse for years before they are married, and yet over lunch two CPAs decide to consummate a business merger.

When a firm is acquiring another firm, the question arises of whether there should be a de-merger agreement. This chapter addresses this issue and, in certain situations, one can see the value of having such an agreement. For example, if A acquires B and then A decides immediately to merge upstream, B would have a right to de-merge within a certain period (preferably two years).

If your firm decides to de-merge into different practices, you may want to refer to the sample dissolution agreement. If this situation occurs, be very careful in notifying your professional liability insurance carrier so that both firms can obtain coverage. I have seen firms split up without addressing this issue, and these firms now have no professional liability insurance.

There are two points of view regarding de-merger provisions. One theory is that if two firms proceed with a business marriage (merger) you should not give one a way out if it does not work. Is this realistic? Prenuptial agreements are frequently used in people's personal lives; the potential for divorce today in a business partnership is always present, so that a de-merger provision should be included to protect the acquired firm. If someone spends 10 years building a firm and decides to be acquired by another firm, the acquired firm should have a de-merger provision in the agreement that will allow the individuals to withdraw from the firm. Generally, the de-merger provision stays in force for a period of two years.

The opposite view is that acquiring a practice is an investment. Normally, the acquired firm closes out its firm and keeps the cash and receivables; thus, the purchaser is financing the acquisition and will not realize any cash profits for the first six months. In other words, it has made an investment. These are major reasons why large firms do not particularly care for de-merger agreements.

There is an alternative. Some firms have a de-merger provision to the effect that after two years there can be a de-merger, but any increase in volume that has occurred during the two-year period represents a fee that must be paid to the surviving firm. In other words, if firm A was generating $1 million in revenue when it merged with Firm B and Firm A left two years later with fees aggregating $1.2 million, Firm A would have to pay Firm B $200,000 over a period of years.

Finally, it is very important to review the partnership agreement to determine what would happen if the merger did not work. If there was no de-merger provision, then one must review the provision relating to partnership termination.

Sample Form

DISSOLUTION AGREEMENT

THIS AGREEMENT, made as of the ———— of ————, by, between and among ————, and ————, a partnership formed under the laws of ————.

W I T N E S S E T H:

WHEREAS, ————, a partnership formed under the laws of the ———— of ———— (the "Partnership"), was formed on ————, whose members consisted of ————, which Partnership was joined by ———— on ———— (———— are sometimes collectively referred to herein as the "Partners"); and

WHEREAS, ————, a partnership formed under the laws of the ———— of ————, was the predecessor to the Partnership and whose members consisted of ————; and

WHEREAS, a portion of the capital contributions of ———— to the Partnership consisted of the assets of ————; and

WHEREAS, to the extent described herein, the Partners wish to dissolve the Partnership and form two partnerships; and

WHEREAS, the Partners agree that the division of the assets and liabilities of the Partnership as set forth herein accurately reflects the relative values of the interests of the Partners in the Partnership.

NOW, THEREFORE, IN CONSIDERATION of the premises and mutual promises herein contained, the parties hereto, intending to be legally bound hereby, do covenant and agree as follows:

1. *Division of Partnership.*

As described herein, the Partnership shall be dissolved effective as of midnight ———— (the "Effective Date") and shall be divided into two partnerships whose members shall consist of ———— and ————, respectively.

2. *Distribution of Partnership*
   a. *Office Furniture.*

The office furniture situated as the offices of the Partnership in the ———— set forth on Schedule A to be attached hereto shall be distributed to _____. All other office furniture situated as the offices of the Partnership in the _____ shall be distributed to _____. It is understood that the items of office furniture normally used by each Partner during the life of the Partnership will be distributed to that Partner.

b. *Equipment.*

The items of equipment set forth on Schedule B to be attached hereto shall be distributed to _____. _____ agrees to assume all rights and liabilities of the Partnership in connection with such items of equipment. The remaining items of equipment shall be distributed to _____. _____ agrees to assume all rights and liabilities of the Partnership in connection with such items of equipment. It is understood that the items of equipment normally used by each Partner during the life of the Partnership will be distributed to that Partner. It is further understood that the word processor and the computer will be distributed to _____.

c. *Library.*

The publications presently contained in the library of the Partnership set forth on Schedule C to be attached hereto shall be distributed to _____. All other publications shall be distributed to _____. The parties to which such publications are distributed agree to assume any liabilities in connection with such publications and to be charged with the value of any prepaid subscriptions.

d. *Other Assets.*

The client records and personnel records listed on Schedule D to be attached hereto (or copies thereof) shall be distributed to _____. _____ will be entitled to reasonable access to such records as good accounting practices or personnel matters may require. _____ shall have reasonable access to accounting records during the period they were Partners.

3. *Accounts Receivable and Payable.*

Each Partner will evaluate the accounts receivable and work in process initially generated by him and will prepare a list of accounts receivable deemed to be uncollectable showing the client and the amount deemed uncollectable and a list of unbilled work in process. Each partner will deliver such lists to each of the other Partners no later than the close of business on _____. The lists of uncollectable accounts receivable will be consolidated as Schedule E to be attached hereto, and the lists of unbilled work in process will be consolidated as Schedule F to be attached hereto. Such Schedules will be subject to approval of all the Partners, which approval shall be noted on such Schedules.

The Liquidating Partner shall open a checking account to be entitled the "Liquidating Account." All cash on hand on the date hereof shall be transferred from the Partnership cash accounts into the Liquidating Account. All sums received from clients of the Partnership with respect to work done on or before _____ shall be deposited by the Liquidating Partner in the Liquidating Account. The Liquidating Account shall remain in existence until sufficient cash has been deposited in said account to accomplish the following:

a. The payment when due of accounts payable attributable to the Partnership and not otherwise assumed by any of the Partners pursuant to the terms of this Agreement.

b. The payment of cash to individual Partners so that (i) the agreed upon value of the assets distributed to the individual Partners under Paragraph 2 hereof and (ii) the value of the accounts receivable and work in process as reflected on Schedule F allocated to the individual Partners hereunder and (iii) all adjustments to the capital accounts of the Partners can be made.

Upon the final distribution, all distributions made pursuant hereto shall, in the aggregate, have been made in accordance with the individual Partners' capital accounts as shown on the final Partnership Balance Sheet.

Amounts received from any client of the Partnership, including any client who continues as a client either of _____ or _____, will be first applied to amounts owing to the Partnership. Prior to the termination of the Liquidating Account, whenever any Partner at any time receives any receipt attributable to the Partnership, he will immediately deliver such amount to the Liquidating Partner in such form that the Liquidating Partner can deposit such amount in accordance with this paragraph.

After termination of the Liquidating Account, all accounts receivable and amounts attributable to work in process unbilled at the date hereof will be distributed to the Partners who initially generated such account, as shown on the Client List to be attached hereto as Schedule G.

4. *Consent of Creditors.*

The Partners agree to take all steps necessary to secure the consent of creditors of the Partnership, including but not limited to the Landlord, to the assumption of liabilities by any Partner according to the terms of the Agreement. In the event that such consent is not obtained as to any such assumption, the Partner(s) who have assumed such liability agree to indemnify and hold the other Partners harmless from any loss in connection with the liabilities assumed.

5. *Lines of Credit.*

Any lines of credit presently available to the Partnership will be terminated   as   of   the   date   hereof   by   delivery   to

_____ of a notice in the form attached as Schedule H.

6. *Payments on Behalf of Partners or Employees.*

No payments shall be made out of funds attributable to the Partnership for any club memberships of any of the Partners for any period after the date hereof. No payments shall be made out of funds attributable to the Partnership for any employee benefit or expense of any of the Partners or any employee of the Partnership for any period after the date hereof. At or before the close of business on _____, each Partner and any employee claiming expenses owed to him by the Partnership shall submit to _____, present office manager of the Partnership, a list in the form and manner heretofore employed by the Partnership, of all unreimbursed expenses attributable to any period prior to the date hereof. Expenses not submitted by such date shall be conclusively presumed to be personal expenses not reimbursable by the Partnership. _____ shall retain the health, life and disability insurance policies presently maintained by the Partnership for its employees. No payments shall be made by _____ for the benefit of any Partner or Partnership employee who does not remain with _____ after the date hereof. _____ shall retain the Federal Employer Identification Number, workmen's compensation rating and unemployment compensation rating of the Partnership.

7. *Charges against Partnership*

Any charges attributable to the Partnership prior to the Effective Date shall be apportioned among the Partners in accordance with the Profit Participation Percentages. If any Partner receives notice of such charge, such notice shall be delivered to the Liquidation Partner, who shall notify each Partner of the amount owed by such Partner. Such amounts shall be delivered to the Liquidating Partner who shall promptly remit such charges to the person to whom such charges are owing.

8. *Preparation of Partnership Tax Returns.*

_____ will prepare and upon approval of all the Partners cause to be filed on behalf of the Partnership any federal, state and local Partnership tax returns required to be filed.

9. *Preparation of Schedules and Balance Sheets.*

Schedules A (Furniture), B (Equipment) and C (Publications) will be completed and delivered to each Partner no later than the close of business on _____. All other Schedules will be completed and delivered no later than the close of business on _____. As soon thereafter as possible, the Liquidating Partner will prepare an Interim Balance

Sheet. Upon the termination of the Liquidating Account, the Liquidating Partner will prepare a Final Balance Sheet for the Partnership. All Schedules, the Interim Balance Sheet and the Final Balance Sheet are subject to approval of the Partners, which approval will be noted on each document.

10. *Telephone Number and Address.*

It is agreed that _____ will retain the telephone number and main office address of the Partnership. Employees of _____ will refer to _____ all mail and telephone calls to _____ or any Partnership employee who becomes employed by _____.

11. *Publications of Notice of Dissolution.*

Within ten days after the date hereof, the Parties hereto will publish an announcement of the dissolution of the Partnership in the _____ Legal Journal and in a newspaper of general circulation in each of _____; and will mail copies of such announcement to creditors, suppliers and other persons and firms which have frequently dealt with the Partnership. No such notice need be sent to clients. The Partners will share equally all expenses in connection with such publication and mailing.

The announcement shall be in substantially the following form:

_____ a Partnership formed under the laws of the _____ of _____ announces that the members to the _____ Partnership have agreed to dissolve the Partnership and to form the firms:

_____

_____

12. *Liquidating Partner.*

_____ is hereby designated the "Liquidating Partner" to act for the Partnership in all matters concerning the winding up of the affairs of the Partnership.

13. *Entire Agreement.*

This Agreement constitutes the entire agreement and understanding of the parties with respect to the subject matter hereof and there are no terms other than those expressly set forth herein. This Agreement completely supersedes and extinguishes all prior negotiations, representations, understandings and/or agreements with respect to the subject matter hereof which are in any way inconsistent herewith.

14. *Further Instruments.*

From and after the date hereof, the Partners agree to execute and deliver such instruments, documents and other writings and do such further acts as may be necessary to vest title to assets in the Partner to whom such assets have been distributed hereunder and otherwise to fully effectuate the intent and purposes of the Partners pursuant to this Agreement.

15. *Modification.*

This Agreement may not be varied, modified, waived, or rescinded in any way except by a writing signed by all parties hereto. Any attempt to vary, modify, waive or rescind all or any portion of this Agreement which does not strictly comply with the terms of this paragraph shall be void and unenforceable.

16. *Governing Law.*

This Agreement shall be governed by and construed in accordance with the laws of the _____ .

17. *Binding Effect.*

This Agreement shall be binding upon and shall inure to the benefit of the parties hereto and their respective successors and assigns.

18. *Use of Facilities.*

For a period of _____ days after the Effective Date, each Partner will be entitled to make reasonable use of equipment and facilities distributed to any of the other Partners hereunder upon payment of the usual hourly rate for such use. Each Partner will have the right to consult for a reasonable number of hours with any other Partner or employee consulted. All amounts due for services used pursuant to this paragraph will be payable within thirty days of the date of the invoice rendered therefor.

IN WITNESS WHEREOF, the parties hereto have executed the Agreement as of the day and year first above written.

WITNESS: _____
         _____

Questions and Answers

Question: Should managers in the firm that is being acquired execute a covenant not to compete agreement?

Answer: In connection with the noncompete agreement with a management group, it makes good business sense to have managers execute this type of agreement. As you well know, managers become very close to clients and certainly can be in a position to leave and take clients and staff.

Today, everyone is talking about the entrepreneurial spirit. If you look at the statistics regarding AICPA membership, there has been almost a 100 per cent increase from the period 1976 to 1986. In 1976 there were 121,947 members, compared to 240,947 in 1986. This increase represents those members who practice public accounting as well as those in business, industry, and other sectors. This increase also means there are more CPA firms. Therefore, I think it is very important for each firm to function as a business and to implement noncompete agreements for managers. It arises not so much out of the intention of restricting their right to work, but the need to be compensated for lost business.

The agreement would be that if a manager decided to leave, the firm would be reimbursed a certain percentage of gross fees for clients that it continued to service. There could be a different percentage for clients brought in by other partners and another percentage for a client that the manager brought in. I would recommend 125 and 75 per cent respectively.

Additionally, development and training of staff is extremely costly and there should be in the noncompete agreement a provision that if a manager leaves and takes staff, the manager pays a fee equivalent to 25 per cent of the individual's salary (this would probably be the fee you would have to pay a search firm to attract a person of similar expertise and experience). This type of clause is normally not included, but I think it should be.

Postmerger Matters

8

Postmerger Follow-up
Questions and Answers
Confidential Partner Questionnaire
Examples of Announcements

After the merger has been agreed to and the related agreements have been executed, it is time to market the merger in the business community and throughout the firm. In other words, you want to let everyone know externally and internally about the merger and its related benefits. Obviously, the merger between Peat Marwick Mitchell & Company and KMG Main Hurdman received a tremendous amount of publicity, as did the contemplated merger between Price Waterhouse & Company and Deloitte Haskins & Sells. In the September 12th issue of the *Wall Street Journal,* a headline was "PEAT-KMG merger will form a Goliath (Companies' Combination to Result in Worlds Biggest Accounting Firm)."[1] Obviously, this was great publicity. The story described the reason for the merger, the benefits to be derived, and gave annual revenue and other statistical data for both organizations, as well as for the combined firm. Obviously, the writer received the information from the firms, but the firms issued the necessary press releases.

When two CPA firms decide to merge, regardless of size, I recommend that they engage an advertising agency (public relations division) to assist them in dissemination of information about the merger

---

[1] Berton, *Peat-KMG Merger Will Form a Goliath,* Wall St J, Sept 12, 1986, at 6, col 1.

throughout the business community. They are the experts and can be of valuable assistance. Individual announcements of the merger can be mailed to clients, bankers, and other business parties. I always recommend that an ad announcing the merger be placed in the business section of appropriate newspapers. Additionally, it is advisable to have an open house to allow the attendees to meet the new team.

From an internal viewpoint, it is most important that the merger be successful. The best way to accomplish this objective is to have a partner retreat to be attended by partners, and sometimes managers, of both firms. The larger firms normally have annual retreats. In some instances partners of the acquired firm attend the annual firm retreat before the merger has been consummated. This is an excellent opportunity for both parties to get together to discuss unsettled issues and also determine if the chemistry exists. I advocate this practice.

When there is a merger of firms of approximately the same size, it is extremely important to have several meetings of the management group so that communication channels are kept open. Both firms must realize that they are now one firm and operate as such. One excellent technique is to have the partner retreat facilitated by an outside consultant. Before the retreat, each partner completes a confidential questionnaire which is submitted to the facilitator. No one else is able to read the documents (see the sample questionnaire in this chapter). The facilitator reads these reports and determines the existence of any problems which may undermine the marriage. During the retreat, the facilitator proceeds with the following scenario:

1. He or she lets *each firm* discuss the strengths and related weaknesses of the respective firm prior to the merger. Each firm records the information on a flip chart. This information is kept in view of all attendees

2. After each firm has completed this exercise, the facilitator then removes all the charts from the walls and destroys them, stating that the strengths and weaknesses were applicable to the *individual* firms

3. The facilitator then proceeds to discuss the strength and weaknesses of the *combined* firm. The exercise is then continued, in a very positive manner, by listing the strengths and weaknesses of the new firm on a flip chart. This is a extremely effective way to start the team-building approach. As mentioned in Chapter 6, the partners of the combined firms should complete an Interpersonal Working Association Inventory or some other useful profile

The key to any successful marriage is to keep the communication channels open. There should be regular staff meetings and "state-of-the-nation" type reports, and management must always communicate with the professional and support staff.

Following are a checklist of other postmerger considerations, and the confidential questionnaire for partners.

Postmerger Follow-up

After the merger agreement has been finalized, it is essential that attention be given to the following factors:

1. *Notifying personnel.* Bulletins should be sent to staff members, visits should be made to merged-in partners, and meetings should be held to answer questions.

2. *Advertising the merger.* Clients should be notified of the merger, letters and/or announcement cards should be sent to bankers, attorneys, and others with whom the firms have close professional relations.

3. *Complying with state registration requirements.*

4. *Making account changes with the bank.* The bank account should be changed to the new firm name, new checks need to be delivered, and the signatures of personnel authorized to sign on behalf of the firm are required.

5. *Changing or canceling insurance coverage as appropriate.*

6. *Revising stationery.* Letterhead, report covers, business cards, and other working papers may need to be changed.

7. *Adjusting office facilities.* May involve moving or remodeling, changing names on building directory, changing telephone numbers and listings, and/or ordering new equipment.

8. *Attending to personnel matters.* Establish directories of partners and staff with home addresses and telephone numbers. Develop compensation policies and employee benefits such as group insurance, vacation, and sick leave.

9. *Preparing firm manuals.* An administrative manual, auditing manual, accounting and reporting manual, tax manual, and staff manuals are among the special types of manuals and brochures a new firm will need.

10. *Distributing firm publications to staff and clients.*

11. *Scheduling of meetings.* Orientation and training may be necessary for staff and partners.

12.   *Collecting receivables which were contributed to the combined firm.*
13.   *Scheduling of billing adjustments and apportionment of subsequent write-offs.*

Questions and Answers

Question: Would you recommend any policy regarding billing for new partners entering our firm, for example—we are a 10-man firm; and we just acquired a practice with three partners and we want to make sure they share our philosophy and understanding as to value billing?

Answer: This is an excellent point. There should be a billing meeting to make sure there is no misunderstanding regarding billing philosophy, and the three partners who are entering the firm must understand the philosophy of the firm as it relates to billing. This situation should also be discussed before the merger is consummated. I have seen situations where partners liked to bill high with hopes of eventually collecting the fee. They may have a 10 percent write off of accounts receivable. Other firms want to make sure what is billed is collected. In the October, 1986 issue of the practicing CPA, Don Itsvan, a consultant to CPA firms, talked about increased realization through reviewed billings. I thought that the contents of the article were excellent and that every CPA firm should consider implementing the procedure described. He stated, "Draft bills should be prepared by each partner, and be reviewed by the billing committee to determine the final billing amounts. The billing committee has the last word on the amounts in the billing. The purpose is to discourage undue write downs and encourage value billing." (See Itsvan, Increased Realization Through Reviewed Billings. Practicing CPA 3 (Oct 1986).)

Question: Why have you commented at different times in this Manual that an outside consultant should be engaged to assist the CPA firm in proceeding with acquiring a practice?

Answer: Sometimes CPAs feel that they can take care of all their own financial matters. The truth of the matter is that CPAs are sometimes so busy in representing their clients that they don't take care of their own financial matters. My comment is basically geared toward those firms that have never been through the merger process or acquired a practice. CPAs are sometimes naive. I feel that firms should seek outside counsel, as they may be a firm that represents a lifetime's work. For example, a CPA in a major city engaged me to review a practice that the CPA was interested in purchasing. When I reviewed the financial data, a major reason for the increased revenue was a substantial fee paid by a client for the CPA firm's assistance in preparing a brochure for the company. This had absolutely nothing to do with performing accounting services. After my two-hour review, I told the CPA who was interested in purchasing the practice not to proceed with the transaction for the price that the seller wanted. I am positive that this particular CPA would not have noticed the fee received for preparing the brochure. Outside counsel can be objective and assist the CPA firm in many ways.

Confidential Partner Questionnaire

Name:_____

Age:_____

Title:_____

Years of Experience:_____

Present Client Account Volume:_____

New Volume of Business Obtained during 1987:_____

Duties:_____

_____

_____

1. What do you feel is the number one problem facing the firm?

_____

_____

_____

_____

2. How do you feel about the firm's compensation system and do you feel that it is fair?

_____

_____

_____

_____

3. What are the strengths of the firm?

_____

_____

_____

_____

4. What are the weaknesses of the firm?

_____

_____

_____
_____

5. How do you feel compensation should be divided?

_____
_____
_____
_____

6. How do you feel about the firm's direction?

_____
_____
_____
_____

7. Are you satisfied with your present responsibilities?

_____
_____
_____
_____

8. Are you satisfied with your present ownership?

_____
_____
_____
_____

9. a. What are the reasons people want to stay and work for the firm?

_____
_____
_____
_____

   b. What are the reasons people want to leave the firm?

_____
_____
_____
_____

10. What are the three issues causing dissension?

_____
_____

_____

_____

_____

11. Would you complete a management style and assessment profile for the next partner retreat?

    YES_____ NO_____

12. How do you rate your firm with other medium-sized firms in your area?

_____

_____

_____

_____

13. What is your opinion about current firm leadership?

_____

_____

_____

_____

14. What kinds of qualities are you looking for in a leader?

_____

_____

_____

_____

15. Would you prefer management by:
    -Managing partner _____
    -Management by committee _____

16. Are there any provisions in the partnership agreement that should be changed?

    YES_____ NO_____
    If yes, which provisions?

_____

_____

_____

_____

17. Does your firm have a good marketing program and documented plan?

    YES_____ NO_____

What should the firm be marketing?

_____
_____
_____
_____

18. Does the firm have a retirement plan?
    YES_____ NO_____
    If not, would you give up current income for future income?
    YES_____ NO_____
19. Do you get along with your other partners?
    YES_____ NO_____
    If no, why?

_____
_____
_____
_____

20. What is your major strength?

_____
_____
_____

21. What is your major weakness?

_____
_____
_____

Additional comments:

_____
_____
_____
_____
_____
_____
_____

Examples of Announcements

WILLIAM C. STEIN, CPA
PATRICK L. LARMON, CPA
JAMES J. WHITLOCK III, CPA

HAVE FORMED THE FIRM OF

STEIN, LARMON & COMPANY

CERTIFIED PUBLIC ACCOUNTANTS

210 W. 22ND STREET

OAK BROOK, ILLINOIS 60521

920-9748

FORMERLY

WILLIAM C. STEIN & COMPANY

PRANGLEY MARKS & CO.

is pleased to announce the acquisition

of the practice of DenBraber & Lyzenga

and that

Robert N. DenBraber, C.P.A.

and

Robert D. Andriessen, C.P.A.

have become associated with the firm

January 3, 1983   900 Union Bank Building
Grand Rapids, Michigan   (616) 774-9004

Conclusion

9

Conclusion
The Ten Commandments for a Successful Merger
The Top 25 CPA Firms
Additional Readings

Conclusion

Today, we live in a merger-mad society; they are exciting and at the same time frustrating times for making the marriage work.

As noted in the cover story of the June 3, 1985 issue of *Business Week*, "in an era of ever-increasing and ever-bigger mergers, a remarkable number—somewhere between a half and two-thirds—simply don't work." In order for a merger to work, we must learn from past experiences and must take the time, both before and after, to properly plan for a merger or acquisition. I advocate that each firm adopt a merger policy and seek outside counsel and advice to make the merger or acquisition a successful one. I hope that the information in this manual has helped the reader to achieve a better understanding of the merger and acquisition process for CPA firms. A list of suggested readings follows.

Although you will find that the book highlights several important issues to consider, seeking objective, independent counsel is essential. The one point that became clear in writing this book is that the chances for a CPA firm during its lifetime to merge with another firm is an excellent one. Finally, remember that people are the key to making a merger work. Confidence, patience and enthusiasm are needed—along with a pinch of good luck.

The Ten Commandments for a Successful Merger

1. The merger must make sound economic sense for both parties

2. Merger must be reviewed by an outside consultant and an opinion obtained as to the fairness of the merger

3. Merger discussion should take a sufficient amount of time so that all issues have been considered. A period of six months is recommended

4. There must be a shared value of merged partners as to quality of service and professionalism

5. Partners and managers of acquired firm become partners and managers in merged firm. Partners of acquired firm should receive earnings guarantee and unit awards for the first two years

6. Unit awards are distributed to acquired partners based on level of experience and earnings

7. Credit for past experience is given in the firm's retirement plan

8. Staff and management of acquired firm must receive extensive training during the first six months

9. All department heads must be involved in the merger process

10. Partner retreat should be held after documents are executed by the partners

The Top 25 CPA Firms

Following is a chart listing the largest 25 CPA firms in the country ranked by estimated volume. It is refreshing to see names of new firms on the top 25 list. Many are well managed and have a bright future. When you review the list, you will note that the combined revenue for the top 10 firms in the country totals $8.4 billion, whereas the revenue for the 15 next largest CPA firms totals $805 million. Obviously, the amount of business controlled by the larger firms is increasing and they will continue to grow and dominate certain sections of the market. From the information in this chart you can determine the average per partner volume for each of the top 25 firms. This exercise will give you a guide for comparison with your firm. Although there are obviously a number of other factors that enter into a merger discussion, a top firm is not going to merge with a firm that has a low volume per partner, unless there are unusual circumstances. As mentioned earlier, it is extremely important to look at the leadership of a firm and its financial data, and it is very important to merge with a firm with similar philosophies. Although we have only listed the top 25 firms, there are over 46,000 CPA firms in the country and many of these would be excellent merger candidates.

Throughout the history of our profession, second- and third-tier firms frequently have merged with either a Big Eight firm or another second- or third-tier firm. Merging will always be a way of life, and, given the globalization of our economy, second- and third-tier firms may merge to remain competitive. Yes, the Big Eight will get bigger, but there is still a great opportunity for small CPA firms throughout the country to continue to develop their practices both internally and via the merger route.

The following pages contain a brief commentary about each of the 25 firms. In certain cases I have indicated their merger policy based on the results of a survey. Certain firms did not want to publicize their merger policy, but it is safe to say that the majority of the top 25 CPA firms have mergers as part of their strategic business plan. Large firms have always been interested in merging profitable practices which will have an impact on the expansion of their existing offices or help them to enter a new marketplace.

25 LARGEST CPA FIRMS IN THE COUNTRY
(RANKED BY ESTIMATED VOLUME)

	Estimated Annual Fee Income*	Estimated Number of Partners	Estimated Number of Offices	Chairperson or Managing Partner
Arthur Andersen & Co. Chicago World Headquarters 69 W. Washington St. Chicago, IL 60602 (312) 580-0069	$1,513,000,000	1,309	85	Duane Kullberg
Peat Marwick Main 55 East 52nd Street New York, NY 10055 (212) 758-9700	$1,458,000,000	1,871	137	Larry Horner
Ernst & Whinney 2000 National City Centre Cleveland, OH 44114 (216) 961-5000	$1,036,000,000	1,250	115	Ray J. Groves

*U.S.A. Operations Only. Estimated Revenue for 1987.

25 LARGEST CPA FIRMS IN THE COUNTRY
(RANKED BY ESTIMATED VOLUME)

	Estimated Annual Fee Income*	Estimated Number of Partners	Estimated Number of Offices	Chairperson or Managing Partner
Coopers & Lybrand 1251 Avenue of Americas New York, NY 10020 (212) 536-2000	$982,000,000	1,110	96	Peter Scanlon
Price Waterhouse 1251 Avenue of Americas New York, NY 10020 (212) 489-8900	$845,000,000	747	112	Joseph Connor
Arthur Young & Co. 277 Park Avenue New York, NY 10172 (212) 407-1500	$738,000,000	799	93	William L. Gladstone

*U.S.A. Operations Only. Estimated Revenue for 1987.

25 LARGEST CPA FIRMS IN THE COUNTRY
(RANKED BY ESTIMATED VOLUME)

	Estimated Annual Fee Income*	Estimated Number of Partners	Estimated Number of Offices	Chairperson or Managing Partner
Deloitte Haskins & Sells 1114 Avenue of the Americas New York, NY 10036 (212) 790-0500	$701,000,000	800	104	J. Michael Cook
Touche Ross & Co. 1633 Broadway New York, NY 10019-6754 (212) 489-1600	$683,000,000	773	84	Edward Kangas
Laventhol & Horwath 1845 Walnut Street Philadelphia, PA 19103 (215) 299-1600	$325,000,000	458	50	George Bernstein

*U.S.A. Operations Only. Estimated Revenue for 1987.

25 LARGEST CPA FIRMS IN THE COUNTRY
(RANKED BY ESTIMATED VOLUME)

	Estimated Annual Fee Income*	Estimated Number of Partners	Estimated Number of Offices	Chairperson or Managing Partner
Grant Thornton Prudential Plaza 39th Floor Chicago, IL 60601 (312) 856-0001	$206,000,000	371	58	Burt Fischer
Seidman & Seidman 15 Columbus Circle New York, NY 10023 (212) 765-7500	$140,000,000	313	49	John Abernathy
McGladrey & Pullen Capital Square Suite 640 Fourth & Locust Street Des Moines, Iowa 50309 (515) 284-8660	$135,000,000	391	57	Jack Whalig

*U.S.A. Operations Only. Estimated Revenue for 1987.

25 LARGEST CPA FIRMS IN THE COUNTRY
(RANKED BY ESTIMATED VOLUME)

	Estimated Annual Fee Income*	Estimated Number of Partners	Estimated Number of Offices	Chairperson or Managing Partner
Kenneth Leventhal & Company 2049 Century Park East Los Angeles, CA 90067 (213) 277-0880	$110,000,000	61	12	Kenneth Leventhal & Stan Ross
Pannell Kerr Forster 624 S. Grand Avenue Suite 1800 Los Angeles, CA 90017 (213) 680-0900	$97,000,000	174	37	Charles Kaiser
Spicer & Oppenheim One New York Plaza New York, NY 10004 (212) 422-1000	$70,000,000	101	11	Donald Tannenbaum

*U.S.A. Operations Only. Estimated Revenue for 1987.

25 LARGEST CPA FIRMS IN THE COUNTRY
(RANKED BY ESTIMATED VOLUME)

	Estimated Annual Fee Income*	Estimated Number of Partners	Estimated Number of Offices	Chairperson or Managing Partner
Baird, Kurtz & Dobson P.O. Box 1900 901 St. Louis St. Springfield, MO 65801 (417) 831-7283	$35,500,000	102	23	James Glauser
Plante & Moran P.O. Box 307 Southfield, MI 48037 (313) 352-2500	$35,000,000	70	11	Edward Parks
Crowe Chizek & Co. P.O. Box 7 South Bend, IN 46624 (219) 236-8677	$28,000,000	67	7	Ronald Cohen

*U.S.A. Operations Only. Estimated Revenue for 1987.

25 LARGEST CPA FIRMS IN THE COUNTRY
(RANKED BY ESTIMATED VOLUME)

	Estimated Annual Fee Income*	Estimated Number of Partners	Estimated Number of Offices	Chairperson or Managing Partner
Cherry Bekaert & Holland 2550 Charlotte Plaza Charlotte, NC 28244 (704) 377-3741	$ 28,000,000	75	22	Gary Wolfe
Moss Adams 2830 Bank of California Center Seattle, WA 98164 (206) 223–1820	$ 27,000,000	54	15	Robert Bunting
Clifton Gunderson & Co. 808 Commercial National Bank Bldg. Peoria, IL 61602 (309) 671-4560	$ 26,000,000	75	25	Curt Mingle
Altschuler, Melvoin and Glasser 30 South Wacker Drive				

*U.S.A. Operations Only. Estimated Revenue for 1987.

25 LARGEST CPA FIRMS IN THE COUNTRY
(RANKED BY ESTIMATED VOLUME)

	Estimated Annual Fee Income*	Estimated Number of Partners	Estimated Number of Offices	Chairperson or Managing Partner
Chicago, IL 60606 (312) 207-2800	$ 23,000,000	33	2	Howard Stone
J.H. Cohn & Company 75 Eisenhower Parkway Roseland, NJ 07068-1697 (201) 228-3500	$ 23,000,000	35	4	Eli Hoffman
Richard A. Eisner & Company 380 Madison Avenue New York, NY 10017 (212) 949-4000	$ 20,000,000	30	1	Richard Eisner
Mann Judd Landau 230 Park Ave., 17th Floor New York, NY 10169 (212) 661-5500	$ 19,000,000	44	8	William Landau

*U.S.A. Operations Only. Estimated Revenue for 1987.

Arthur Andersen & Co.

Arthur Andersen & Co. is still the largest and one of the most profitable CPA firms in the country. They have been well regarded as the businessman's firm because of their expertise and heavy concentration in the management advisory service area. They have the second smallest number of offices of the Big Eight, but yet the most revenue. They have always built substantial bases in major cities, far surpassing the revenue of existing firms that have been in a city a long time. They are a very aggressive firm, and the major part of their growth has been internal. They have the highest volume per partner, in excess of $1 million. Except in cases of firms with expertise in the MAS area or with a product that has been developed within the firm, or firms with a significant average per partner income, Arthur Andersen would probably not be interested in merging. They are a very advanced in the development of products and recently established a new technical service organization which is responsible for the development of information technology. Although they have had large settlements in litigation, they are exceptionally well managed, and continue to be a dominant firm in the marketplace.

Peat Marwick Main

Peat Marwick Main is now the largest firm in the world, as a result of the recent merger between Peat Marwick Mitchell & Co. and KMG Main Hurdman. This was a merger combining the second and ninth largest CPA firms in the country. It is interesting to note that Peat Marwick Mitchell and Klynveld Main Goerdelar engaged in merger discussions a few years ago, but these were terminated because of substantial cultural differences. We all can remember in 1977 when two large firms, J.K. Lasser and Touche Ross & Co., merged, and this presented many difficulties because of cultural and philosophical differences. In any substantial merger there is normally a period of three years required to settle the waves and for people to learn to work together as a team. It takes strong leadership to make such a merger effective and certain decisions will have to be made by terminating frustrated partners and others who are not running on the same track. Peat Marwick Main has the leadership to make the merger work. The interesting aspect of this merger is that it will certainly make the other Big Eight firms and second-tier firms think more about the necessity to merge to expand their competitiveness in serving an international client base.

KMG Main Hurdman growth had long been mergers, as the firm was a combination of Main LaFrentz, Hurdman Cranstoun Penny & Co., John F. Forbes and several other firms.

In 1985 the *Wall Street Journal* had reported that Peat Marwick Mitchell asked about 5 per cent of their partners to leave in a cost-cutting move. From 1985 to 1987, they reorganized and developed their plan for the future, which obviously included the merger with KMG Main Hurdman. They are certainly a dominant firm and will continue to develop their MAS and specialty type practices through acquisitions. As are other Big Eight firms, they are interested in merging with excellent practices in areas where they would like to expand their practice or which will enable them to enter a new marketplace. With the recent merger, they now have the most offices of any of the top 25 CPA firms in the country, which will provide them with an excellent base to market all their services.

Ernst & Whinney

The firm was founded in 1903 and has offices in all states. In the pattern of most of the Big Eight firms they have grown internally; however, acquisitions are part of their strategic plan. They are interested not only in general practices, but also in specialty type practices with expertise in health care, financial institutions, tax, and consulting services. When they are acquiring a practice they are interested in the following considerations: quality of practice, growth potential, and industry expertise. The firm has been noted for services in the health care and financial institution markets. They found a niche many years ago and have been able to build on that expertise especially in view of expanded services to the health care community. When one looks at the future requirements in the health care industry, this firm has positioned itself well for continued growth. Although they are a firm that has basically grown internally, they will merge to establish themselves in a market, as they did when they merged with S.D. Leidsdorf. I would not be surprised if this excellent firm merged with another Big Eight firm, such as Arthur Young, which would make them the second largest accounting firm in the world.

Coopers & Lybrand

The firm was founded in 1898 and has offices throughout the country. They have 15 offices in the East, 42 in the West, 8 in the North, and 30 in the South. During the past three years they have consummated four mergers. The firm has excellent leadership and will continue its pattern of outstanding growth. The majority of their growth has been internal; however, acquisitions of CPA firms are part of their strategic plan. Their present volume per partner is approximately $875,000. They have had excellent growth in their MAS practice. They are interested in firms that will provide them with a major impact in certain sections of the country.

Price Waterhouse

The firm is one of the most profitable CPA firms in the country. They are one of the three Big Eight firms whose name has remained the same over the past 50 years. The firm has grown internally, and has only merged with firms that gave them stronger presence in an area or had a specialty type practice. The firm has consummated five mergers during the last three years and acquisitions are part of their strategic plan. They are interested in acquiring firms with a minimum gross volume of $1,000,000, or minimum volume per partner of $1,000,000 and a minimum income per partner of $250,000. The quality of partners, quality of practice and potential of geographic area are the key considerations in acquiring a practice. It normally takes at least 12 years to become a partner in the firm. Once someone achieves this goal, they rarely leave this profitable firm. They have excellent leadership at the top and recently decided to reduce their regions from eleven to five. I would not be surprised if Deloitte Haskins & Sells and Price Waterhouse went back to the altar. In 1984, both firms wanted the merger. The merger was vetoed by partners in the United Kingdom, but perhaps recent events, such as the Peat, Marwick Main combination, can change their minds. The firms' globalization and servicing of world markets is very competitive. Because of the global aspect of the business environment I think that the consolidation of these two firms will occur, which would result in an excellent organization with solid leadership.

Arthur Young & Co.

The firm is one of the three Big Eight firms in the country whose name has not changed during the last 50 years. It is basically a firm that has grown internally, but recently decided that they want to enter the market serviced by local firms. In July, 1986 they acquired May Zima, a large Florida-based firm. Their entrepreneurial service group is now interested in penetrating this market and adding to the growth of the firm. Their present strategy is to acquire local firms to help them get small, fast-growing companies as clients. In the February, 1988 issue of *Bowman's Accounting Report,* the National Director of Entrepreneurial Services Group (ESG) for Arthur Young stated "that they were looking for medium sized local firms with approximately twenty to forty staff to add a high degree of sophistication in business advisory service, micro installation, business planning, and financial assistance." They are interested in merging with firms in metropolitan areas where their ESG group is not as well established. They have recently released data about firm operations for the first time, and are making various business decisions that include closing offices in certain parts of the country. I would not be surprised if they merged with another Big Eight firm, such as Ernst & Whinney.

Deloitte Haskins & Sells

Deloitte & Co. was founded in England in 1845, and Haskins & Sells began in the United States in 1895. In 1978 the name was changed to Deloitte Haskins & Sells. The firm has an excellent reputation for quality service and professionals. The firm has a large number of SEC clients and in 1983 made many changes as a result of their strategic business plan. During that period they reorganized and elected a new management team, which has resulted in excellent growth. They have positioned themselves to take advantage of their excellent expertise in certain industries, particularly in dealing with the public offering and SEC markets. They are interested in merging with firms that give them additional presence in a city or in a new area. During the last three years the firm has consummated twelve mergers. The three most important considerations they look for in acquiring a practice are its "quality," the expertise of the firm, and the attractiveness of the market in terms of growth and profitability. The firm is a very young partnership with a great deal of enthusiasm and talent. They recently completed mergers in Chicago and Virginia that helped improve their current position and visibility in those areas. The managing partner is well respected and is an excellent leader. Under his leadership the firm will continue to grow both from a gross volume and earnings viewpoint.

Touche Ross & Co.

The firm is the eighth largest CPA firm in the country and is challenging Deloitte Haskins & Sells and Arthur Young & Co. for seventh and sixth places, respectively. It has merged with many firms throughout the country. They estimate that their gross revenue for 1988 will be $800 million. Their former managing partner, Russell Palmer, orchestrated its successful growth, although not without pain. They were able to survive the J.K. Lasser merger by adopting a tough stances and making tough decisions regarding partner withdrawals and defections. They recently have had excellent growth not only in gross volume, but also in earnings. They service the middle market exceptionally well.

The firm grew by adopting a merger policy and, although they had some failures, they have certainly demonstrated the ability to grow not only by the merger route, but also internally by creating a synergistic philosophy. They have consummated approximately 10 mergers during the last three years, and acquisitions are part of their strategic plan. They are interested in acquiring specialty practices. When they acquire a practice, the three most important considerations are specialty areas, profits, and quality of people. They serve as a model for those second- and third-tier firms that want to establish themselves throughout the country by the merger route. I will not be surprised if, within two years, this firm becomes the sixth largest CPA firm in the country, providing there are no further mergers between Big Eight Firms.

Laventhol & Horwath

The firm was founded in 1915 and has offices in 25 different states with 16 offices in the East, 10 in the West, 16 in the North, and 8 in the South. During the past three years, they have consummated 27 mergers; and obviously acquisitions are part of their strategic plan. The firm has grown through the merger route and internally. They are interested in general practices or specialty type practices with emphasis in real estate, health care, and leisure time industries. They have no specific minimums regarding gross volume and minimum volume per partner. They are interested in firms in all geographic locations. Their estimated revenue for 1988 is $375 million. The three most important considerations they look for when merging a practice are the quality of the practice, talent of the particular individuals, and the potential for synergistic growth. They have an outstanding managing partner. I would not be surprised if they merged with another second-tier firm in the next few years, which would place them in the position of a contender for one of the Big Eight positions.

Grant Thornton

The firm has 68 offices located throughout the country, and has grown both internally and via the merger route. They are interested in acquiring firms that can give them additional presence in new cities or enhance their present location. They are looking for a per partner volume of between $500,000 and $600,000. They are obviously interested in firms that have quality people, industry expertise, and good economics. The firm experienced a decrease in revenue from 1986 to 1987 and also had adverse publicity regarding a legal situation. They are diligently working to overcome this negative publicity and also making changes to enhance the bottom line. I would not be surprised if Grant Thornton decided to merge with another second-tier firm or with a

Big Eight firm. In 1979 there were preliminary discussions held between Alexander Grant & Company and Laventhel & Horwath, but they were subsequently terminated.

Seidman & Seidman

The firm was founded in 1910 and has 49 practice offices located throughout the country, with 7 located in the Northeast, 12 located in the West and Southwest, 11 in the Midwest, and 9 located in the Southeast. They are one of the few second-tier firms that still has their original name. During 1985, 1986, and 1987, the firm consummated 19 mergers. Mergers have constituted approximately 30 to 40 per cent of the firm's annual growth. Their estimated volume for 1988 is $160 million. Acquisitions have always been part of their strategic plan. They are interested both in general practices and in specialty type practices with expertise in actuarial, executive search, personal and financial planning, corporate financing, and financial consulting services. They are interested in firms with a minimum annual gross volume of $1 million, a minimum volume per partner of $350,000, and minimum income per partner of $100,000. They are interested in firms in all geographic locations. When they are considering merging a practice, the three most important considerations are compatible practice philosophy, satisfactory strategic planned objectives, and profitability. The firm has strong leadership and within a few years will be one of the top 10 firms in the country.

McGladrey & Pullen

The firm has approximately 57 offices in 16 states. In 1984, McGladrey Henderickson and A.M. Pullen merged and they have spent the last four years solidifying the merger. The firm's new name became effective on May 1, 1988. The firm has always been interested in mergers that will enhance present offices and now is prepared to move ahead after solidifying their recent merger. They are interested in merging with CPA firms with an average volume per partner of $350,000. The firm offers CPA firms that are not interested in merging with the opportunity to join their network. Each firm that joins the network receive all McGladrey resources which include technical, management, and educational materials. The fee is based on annual billings. They are an interesting firm that has no present aspiration to become a national firm. However, they offer a choice for well-managed medium sized firms either to merge or join their network.

Kenneth Leventhal & Company

The firm was founded in 1948 and has two offices located in the East, five in the West, two in the North, and three in the South. Their estimated gross revenue for 1988 is $118 million. The majority of their growth has been strictly internal. During the last three years they have consummated only one merger. However, acquisitions are part of their strategic plan. The firm is interested in specialty type practices servicing the real estate or financial institution markets. They are interested in firms with a minimum gross volume of $2 million and a minimum volume per partner of $500,000. The three most important considerations they look for in merging with a firm are potential growth through synergism, skills and work attitude of the partners, and staff and extent of support needed from the executive office. In Mark Stevens book entitled *The Accounting Wars,* the firm was listed as the most profitable of all the large CPA firms. The firm operates with a nominal executive office staff. They have most of their CPE geared to the technical subjects, and the partners have a high number of charge hours. They are an extremely well managed and profitable firm.

Pannell Kerr Forster

The firm was founded in 1911 and has 37 practice offices throughout the country, with 8 located in the East, 12 in the West, 5 in the North, and 12 in the South. During the past three years the firm has consummated 25 mergers and the majority of their firm's growth has been internal as well as via the merger route. Obviously, acquisitions are still part of their strategic plan. The firm's estimated revenue for U.S. operations in 1988 is $110,000,000. They are interested in firms with either a general practice or specialty type practices, and the gross volume requirement depends upon whether a firm is a stand-alone office or located in a city with existing office. They are interested in firms with a minimum volume per partner of $750,000 and a minimum income per partner of $150,000 in all geographic locations throughout the country. Their three most important considerations in acquiring a practice are, does it help the clients, does it make more money for the firm, and will it provide better opportunities for the professional staff. This firm has recently elected a new managing partner after 15 years under the leadership of Mr. Kaiser. With new leadership, there will certainly be organizational changes.

Spicer & Oppenheim

This firm was founded approximately 35 years ago, and has offices located in New York, Florida, Texas, Colorado, California, and Illinois. Because of their international affiliation, the firm name was changed from Oppenheim Appel Dixon & Company to the current name in January, 1988. They have several public clients and do an extensive amount of SEC work. They have grown internally, but have merged with other practices that have given them a presence in areas where they have opened an office. Their only start-up operation was in Los Angeles. They are making necessary changes within the firm to position themselves for future growth. The firm has had excellent growth since its inception. With the recent international merger there will certainly be additional changes in the firm operation. Because of the nature of their practice, I would not be surprised if they merged with one of the Big Eight.

Baird Kurtz & Dobson

The firm was founded in 1923, and has grown significantly during the last 10 years, with offices in Arkansas, Kansas, Kentucky, Missouri, Nebraska, Oklahoma, Tennessee, and Texas. The firm has had a history of successful mergers, has excellent leadership, and has doubled their growth during the last five years. They have increased their professional staff from 263 in 1980 to 590 in 1987. Their estimated revenue for 1988 is $44 million. They have consummated 15 mergers through 1985, 1986, and 1987. Their growth has been both internal and via the merger route. They are interested in acquiring firms with a general practice or a specialty type practice in health care, transportation, financial institutions, consulting, or manufacturing. They are interested in firms with a minimum annual gross volume of $1 million for a new location. There is no limit for existing office locations. They are interested in firms with a minimum volume per partner of $300,000 and a minimum income per partner of $75,000. They are interested in firms located in the Central and South Central parts of the country. The three most important considerations they look for in merging a practice are compatibility of personnel with existing firm personnel, quality of workmanship, and the desire to become part of the continuing organization. The firm has grown in a very organized manner and is one of the fastest growing firms in the country.

Plante, Moran

The firm was founded in 1935 and has 11 offices located in the Northern part of the United States, with executive office located in Michigan. During the last three years, they completed three mergers. Their growth has been internal as well as by the merger route. The firm is interested in merging with general practices or specialty type practices with health care, real estate, or actuary and employee benefit expertise. They are interested in merging with firms that have a minimum annual gross volume of $1 million, a minimum volume per volume of $400,000, and a minimum income per partner of $85,000. They are interested in merging with firms in the Northern part of the country. Their anticipated gross revenue for 1988 is $38 million. The three most important characteristics they look for in merging a practice are: excellent accounts and growth potential from these accounts, excellent people (partners and staff), and a geographic location that fits in with their other locations. The firm is a strong third-tier firm, one with very good leadership.

Crowe Chizek & Company

The firm was founded in 1942, and has 7 offices located in Indiana, Michigan, Ohio, and Illinois. Their estimated volume for 1988 is $39 million. They have consummated two mergers during the past three years. The majority of their growth has been internal; however, acquisitions are part of their strategic plan. They are interested in firms located in the East, North, or South with a general or specialty practice in health care, manufacturing, or financial institutions. They are interested in firms with a minimum volume per partner of $500,000. The three most important considerations they look for in merging a practice are people, type of client base, and profitability of practice. In 1986, they consummated their initial merger, which has been very successful, and since then have merged another practice. They are an extremely well managed firm with excellent leadership. They have positioned the firm for substantial growth during the next five years.

Cherry Bekaert & Holland

The firm has the majority of their offices located in the south. They recently completed their fiscal year and had a substantial 28 per cent increase in gross revenue. The firm has 500 professional staff, including 75 partners. They have had an excellent year and have positioned themselves well for growth in other sectors of the country. Although they have 22 offices, they do not have an executive office, as their expertise in certain areas is located in various practice offices. They recently completed a merger in Richmond, Virginia. They are generally interested in practices with a gross volume of $750,000 and a per partner volume of $350,000. They are also a firm that has grown via the merger route. They have done an outstanding job in developing marketing materials, such as the development of brochures for various industries. This firm will continue to expand to other sections of the country.

Moss Adams

The firm was founded in 1913 and has 15 offices located in the Western part of the country. They estimate that their gross revenue for 1988 will exceed $30 million. They have consummated six mergers during the past three years. Despite these mergers, most of their growth has been internal. They are interested in merging with firms with general practices as well as specialty practices. They are primarily interested in firms with a minimum annual gross volume of $1 million and a minimum volume per partner of $425,000. Future mergers are part of their strategic business plan. They are interested in continuing to merge or acquire firms located in the West. When considering a merger, the three important considerations are the quality of the personnel, the location of the office, and the quality of the clients. Moss Adams is a well managed firm.

Clifton Gunderson & Company

The firm was founded in 1960. They have 25 practice offices. Two are located in the East, 4 in the West, and 19 in the Midwest. The firm estimates that revenue for the current year will be $33 million. They are a firm that has grown both internally and through mergers. During the past three years they have consummated seven mergers. Acquisitions are part of their strategic plan and they are interested in acquiring general practices and specialty type practices with health care, financial services, and general MAS expertise. They are interested in firms with a minimum annual volume of $750,000 in a new city, and a minimum volume per partner of $300,000. They are interested in all geographic locations. The three most important considerations in acquiring a practice are talent of individuals, philosophy of practice, and commitment to quality growth. This is another example of how a firm has grown via the merger route by establishing a game plan for acquisitions.

Altschuler, Melvoin and Glasser

The firm was founded in 1923, and presently has two offices—one in the West and one in the North. For years they operated out of their Chicago office and during the last three years they consummated one merger. Obviously, the majority of the firm's growth has been internal, but acquisitions are part of their strategic plan. They are interested in acquiring general practices and specialty type practices with expertise in manufacturing and health care. They are interested in firms with a minimum annual gross volume of $1 million, minimum volume per partner of $500,000, and minimum income per partner of $100,000 in all geographic locations. When acquiring a practice they are interested in the following three considerations: quality people with special skills, clients/specialty area where potential for growth exists, and geographic location in favorable growth area to enable them to complement/add to existing locations or expand into new areas. The firm's estimated revenue for the current year is $29 million. The firm is extremely well managed and has a director of operations who was very instrumental in the significant growth of another CPA firm. They have demonstrated the ability to grow internally in a very organized manner and, like other firms, have decided to expand via the merger route.

J.H. Cohn & Co.

The firm commenced operation in 1938 and has four offices in New Jersey and one in San Diego, California. The firm has over 300 professionals and are a very well-organized and managed firm. They have an extensive SEC practice. They have recently admitted the Director of Human Resources to partnership, which certainly is a indication of their commitment to recruiting and developing outstanding individuals. They have a quality practice with excellent people.

Richard A. Eisner & Company

The firm was founded in 1963, and has one office in New York City—is one of the largest single firm offices in the country for a non-Big Eight firm. They have not consummated any mergers during the last three years. Their estimated gross volume for 1988 is $25 million. Their growth has been strictly internal; however, as part of their strategic plan, they have an interest in acquiring firms. They are interested in specialty type practices regarding entertainment, management consulting, and personal financial planning. They have no minimum volume per partner for interested firms. They are very interested in firms located on the East Coast. The three most important considerations they look at in acquiring a practice are people, specialties, and type of clients. The firm has excellent leadership, as the managing partner is the founding partner. In 25 years they have become one of the top 25 CPA firms in the country, which is quite an accomplishment.

Mann Judd and Landau

The firm has 8 offices and is based in New York City. They are a firm that has grown internally, but recently have consummated a few mergers. They have a quality SEC practice. They recently won a major victory in a professional liability case that will certainly assist the profession in various suits against CPA firms. They are very organized and well managed firm.

Additional Readings

In order to be more aware about this entire subject, we recommend that you read the following articles:

1. *Do Mergers Really Work?*, Bus Wk, June 3, 1985, at 88, col 1.
2. *Merger Gale Blows Over USA Terrain,* USA Today, Jan 27, 1986, at §E, pl, col 4.
3. Lang, *Buying, Merging or Selling an Accounting Practice,* 16 Prac Acct 87 (Nov 1983).
4. Coker, *Some Practical Tips on Buying or Merging an Accounting Practice,* 14 Prac Acct 17 (Mar 1981).
5. Liberty, *To Merge or Not To Merge,* 151 J Acct 52 (Jan 1981).
6. Schwechter & Quintero, *Valuing the Professional Service Corporation,* Equitable Distribution Rep (June 1983).
7. Practitioner Pub Co/AICPA, The Management of an Accounting Practice Handbook ch 107 (1987).
8. Mingle, *Making the Marriage Last,* vol 8 no 8 Prac CPA 1 (Aug 1984).
9. Knights, *Reaching Common Ground on Goodwill,* 7 Chartered Acct in Australia 10 (Oct 1984).
10. The Equitable Distribution Reporter, a monthly publication of Aspen Systems, 1600 Research Boulevard, Rockville, Maryland 20850 (Periodically, there is information about valuing an accounting practice in marital disputes).

11. Marks & Mievis *The Merger Syndrome,* Psychology Today, Oct 1986, at 36.

12. Goddard, *Valuing An Accounting Practice (Part 1),* vol 6 no 3 Practicing CPA 7 (March 1982).

13. Goddard, *Valuing An Accounting Practice (Part 2),* vol 6 no 4 Practicing CPA 7 (Apr 1982).

14. Sanders, *Purchasing a Small Practice: The Way to Grow Quickly,* vol 10 no 9 Practicing CPA 1 (Sept 1986).

15. Loscalzo, *Checklist for Merger or Acquisition of Professional Firms,* Modern Acct & Auditing Checklist 14.10 (May 1981).

16. Jarrow, *How to Successfully Merge Your Accounting Practice,* 9 Prac Acct 19 (May/June 1976).

17. Jarrow, *How to Successfully Merge Your Accounting Practice,* 19 Prac Acct 70 (Dec 1986).

18. Kaiser, *Mergers: Should You? If So, How?* 21 Prac Acct 71 (Mar 1988).

19. Istvan, *Merger Mania — Why?* vol 9 no 5 Practicing CPA (May 1985).

R.J. GALLAGHER & ASSOCIATES, INC., MERGER AND ACQUISITION QUESTIONNAIRE

Please fill in or circle the correct response.

Part I

1. (a) What is the size of your firm? _____
    (b) What is the size of your professional staff? _____
    (c) How many partners are in your firm? _____
2. What is your gross revenue during the latest fiscal year? _____
3. What state are you located in? _____

Part II

1. Has your firm ever been involved in a merger?   Yes No
    a.   If No, go to Part IV, page 168
    b.   If Yes, answer the following.
         (There may be more than one answer)
         1.   Was it an acquisition?   Yes No
         2.   Was it a lateral merger?   Yes No
         3.   Was it a merger with a larger firm?   Yes No
2. Would you consider another merger?   Yes No
    a.   Lateral   Yes No
    b.   Regional or national   Yes No
    c.   Small   Yes No
3. Why did you merge? (circle as many as are applicable)
    a.   Lack of management succession   Yes No
    b.   High professional liability insurance   Yes No
    c.   Inadequate retirement plan   Yes No
    d.   Stagnant growth   Yes No
    e.   Insufficient resources   Yes No
    f.   Competition   Yes No
    g.   Earnings erosion   Yes No
4. In the merger agreement, was there provision(s) for:
    a.   Payment for goodwill   Yes No
    b.   Upfront cash payment   Yes No
    c.   Convenant not to compete   Yes No
    d.   Back professional liability insurance   Yes No
    e.   Assumption of lease obligations   Yes No

    f.   Earning guarantee   Yes No

    g.   Credit for past employment
        experience in pension plan   Yes No

5. What was the time frame of the merger discussion?

    a.   Over twelve months   Yes No

    b.   Three to six months   Yes No

    c.   Less than three months   Yes No

6. Did you have to obtain back liability
insurance? What was the:

    a.   Premium: _____

    b.   Length of coverage: _____

    c.   Credit: _____

7. If your firm acquired a practice,
how was the purchase price determined?

    a.   Based on subsequent collections   Yes No

    b.   Based on current volume   Yes No

    c.   What percentage of the gross volume?

        1.   25 -50%   Yes No

        2   50 - 75%   Yes No

        3.   75 - 100%   Yes No

        4.   100 - 125%   Yes No

        5.   125 - 150%   Yes No

        6.   Over 150%   Yes No

8. If payment of goodwill was included in the
purchase price, how was it allocated?

    a.   Fixed assets   Yes No

    b.   To client list   Yes No

    c.   Both   Yes No

    d.   Other please state: _____

9. What was the term of payment of indebtedness to
acquire the practice?

    a.   Over 5 years   Yes No

    b.   2 to 5 years   Yes No

    c.   Under 2 years   Yes No

10. What was the interest rate?

    a.   Above prime   Yes No

    b.   Prime   Yes No

    c.   Below prime   Yes No

11. Did you lose any major client within one
year after the merger?   Yes No

12. Did you lose any professional staff
during the first year after the merger?

    a.   100%   Yes No

b.	75 to 100%	Yes	No
c.	50 to 75%	Yes	No
d.	25 to 50%	Yes	No
e.	0 to 25%	Yes	No

13. How many of your professional staff were left after three years?

a.	100%	Yes	No
b.	75 to 100%	Yes	No
c.	50 to 75%	Yes	No
d.	25 to 50%	Yes	No
e.	0 to 25%	Yes	No

14. Did you receive the same fringe benefits with the new firm?   Yes   No

15. If there was a covenant not to compete in your agreement?
    a. Low long   _____
    b. What area   _____
    c. What was the penalty if you left the firm before the covenant expired?

    _____

Part III

1. Was the merger successful?   Yes   No
   a. If No, please check the appropriate reason(s) for failure:

1.	Loss of client	Yes	No
2.	Personality differences	Yes	No
3.	Management Leadership	Yes	No
4.	Treated like second class citizen	Yes	No
5.	Too much family involvement	Yes	No
6.	Unequitable Compensation	Yes	No
7.	Other	Yes	No

      Please state: _____

      _____

Part IV   Please answer the following questions:

1. Has your firm provided adequate funds to pay for partners' retirement?   Yes   No
2. Are you concerned with the increased professional liability insurance premium?   Yes   No
3. In your opinion, where is the future strength

in the accounting profession?

a.	Local firm specializing in certain areas	Yes	No
b.	Medium firm	Yes	No
c.	Regional firm	Yes	No
d.	National firm	Yes	No

4. Would you use an outside consultant to evaluate a potential merger?   Yes   No

5. Does your current partnership agreement have any specific provisions relating to a merger with another firm?   Yes   No

   If so, please comment:

   _____

   _____

   _____

6. Would you consider merging with a:

a.	National firm	Yes	No
b.	Regional firm	Yes	No
c.	Medium firm	Yes	No
d.	Local firm	Yes	No

Name of firm   _____

Address   _____

               _____

               _____

Contact person _____

The author wants to accumulate data relating to merger activity. Each respondent will receive a copy of the results of the survey. However, the survey will not disclose the name of any firm that provides the requested information. Please make a copy of the completed questionnaire and mail to Mr. Robert J. Gallagher, CPA, President, R.J. Gallagher and Associates, Inc., 2445 One Mellon Bank Center, 500 Grant Street, Pittsburgh, PA 15219.

Index

W